Fake
Optimists

Three People to <u>Fire</u>
&
Three People to <u>Hire</u>

By Keith R. Kelsch

Vision Impact Books
St. George, Utah
http://www.visionimpactbooks.org

Published by Keith Kelsch/Vision Impact Books
Distributed by Lulu.com
ISBN 978-0-359-67175-5

To those willing to taste the waters of truth and stem
the tide of a hypocritical world, now is the time of great
knowledge, the kind that is not set to destroy but rather to
quench the thirst of those ready to understand. This book
will not help those who look to control others or to seek
riches of great honor. Instead, this book will help those
willing to correct our misguided thinking about leadership
and how we should organize every business. One might
think God already knows.

Samuel Louis Dael

Table of Contents

Forward

by Richard K. Harder

The Author

One could compare Keith R. Kelsch to a modern-day Socrates who talks about conventional organizations and leadership in a very candid and somewhat disturbing way. He is direct and painfully to the point. He is one of the most widely read authors, educators, and consultants to leaders that I have met.

I met Keith in December of 2017 as he was closing a communications class scheduled just before one of my classes at a prominent Southern Utah university. It became obvious to me that Keith had exceptional drive in his adjunct teaching role. More apparent was the fact that Keith was driven to educate business leaders about how their organizations can thrive by eliminating unnecessary power struggles, hindering bureaucracies, and weak leaders, which he calls fake optimists.

About the Book

This book is clearly not intended to make the reader feel good about the way things are in their organization. It is intended to shake the reader and to create a 180-degree shift in how they run their organization.

The book describes organizational pitfalls in business, government, and even community that will likely make you feel uneasy about the way things have been going for too long. The purpose of the book is to help you become more aware of organizational dysfunction and to kickstart a drive to make a positive change which will require significant transparency and commitment to major changes.

You will likely experience a wide range of emotions as you read this book – anxiety, astonishment, courage, determination, guilt, indignation, pity, reflection, shame and surprise to name a few. Why? Because you will be reading about the "white elephant" everyone is aware of but no one is talking about.

Enjoy this out-of-the-box read. Learn about the testing of new vision, the mechanics of a thriving culture, dysfunctional power struggles, fake personalities, the value of consent, and the immovability of elitism.

Keith provides powerful and disturbing insights on how you can reengineer an organization to increase creativity, productivity, and retention. Most powerful is his vision for humanity, perhaps even a new renaissance many are longing for.

Leaders and founders who stand to be questioned and are willing to be influenced by all corners of the organization will benefit greatly from the insights shared in this book. However, those that are backwardly political, and fake will soon find themselves in the hole they dug for themselves.

Introduction

The word fake is now used everywhere. Fake news, fake leaders, and fake people. Everyone is calling something or someone fake. Since nobody dares to explain what defines a fake person, and since every other popular non-fiction publication is too busy categorizing platitudes of personal success or personal improvement, here we talk about fake people, how to spot them, and why we need to fire them.

I have been told this book is filled with discomfort, at least for the first few chapters. It is never easy to fire anyone. The only thing that makes it easier is to see the damage they are doing to the organization. If you could see this with your own eyes, then firing them should not be that hard. Right?

What is hard is the self-realization that you hired a fake optimist in the first place, or you voted such a person into office under false pretense. You were deceived and this is what is hard to face.

In 2001 James Collins published his national bestseller *Good to Great*. In that book, he found that great leaders get the wrong people off the bus and the right people on the bus. Fake Optimists is written to help you see the wrong people in a way never before communicated.

So, as you read, be prepared to see fake intentions better than ever. It will first require some level of discomfort, as no awakening is without a little cynical realization. It is the best way to see what is genuine on the other side, and trust me when I say this, there is a powerful other side to humanity. I call it the high road.

When one thinks of deep religious concepts, the greatest gift is to read the hearts and minds of individuals. Then again, Jesus Christ would have such a skill as to whom he could call and who he would cast aside. Most of us are hypocritical Fake Optimists. Very few are genuine.

Ronald Kelsch

1

Staged Optimists

Optimism is not a show we perform. When someone makes it a show, that person is on life's stage only to project a fake quality into the audience. This kind of optimism does not entertain, it does not teach, and the actor is not believable.

Samuel Louis Dael

Fake Performances

My first encounter with a staged optimist came in my first year of college while working as a host for a French-cuisine restaurant in Westlake Village, California. It was a fine-dining restaurant where we prepared the food tableside, including fresh Caesar salad with smoked chicken, Dover sole cooked in white wine, and bananas foster fired in sweet liqueur. My uniform was a freshly pressed tuxedo, polished black shoes, and manicured hands; the clientele, for its part, was new money.

The maître d' was Richard, a twenty-eight-year-old handsome MBA graduate from the University of Spoiled Children (a name those at UCLA gave to their rival USC). Favoring UCLA myself, I had a built-in dislike for Richard.

Richard connected with new people, but he never sustained that connection over time. He was the spitting image of Frankie Avalon, the teen heartthrob and singer/actor in the sixties who co-starred in several beach movies with Annette Funicello. With dark curly hair cut short, a small frame, and a tailored tuxedo, Richard had the same transient energy as Frankie. Every moment was a beach party. His first impression was his best impression, which seemed to crash within a week or two of every new relationship.

The floor captain, also called the lead waiter, was just the opposite. His name was Mike and he loved food, and it showed in his happy, blotchy face. Personal and one-on-one, he built a kindred relationship with everybody, especially over time. The more time you spent with him, the richer the relationship became.

The difference between these two men surfaced not so much in the impressions they left as in the abundance in human connection that Mike had and Richard did not. Everyone gravitated toward Richard, while it took more time to know Mike.

First impressions can promote a false optimistic feeling in others. It's like the first time you meet a cotton-candy cheerleader at a high-school football rally: bubbly and delightful at first, but without the deepness of meaning expressed in one's quality of life, these superficial first impressions disappear in time. Eventually, this same person stands naked in front of you in their raw insecurity. This is why a staged optimist eventually evaporates like warm breath in the cold night air. In the cotton-candy analogy, the fun and energy are there—and then they're gone.

This quick disappearance of energy does not describe real optimism. The two men I referenced above taught me this. One lived a life of show; the other lived a life of service. Richard was linear and a packrat for the newest groupie to follow him. Mike was relational and a packhorse always willing to carry a friend. The difference between these two men grew exponentially wider in how they managed people.

When Richard hired me as host, he gave me specific instructions to overbook the reservations and to keep the tables filled—with guests waiting in the hotel lobby. The reservations were booked exactly as he told, but at a loss of quality service. Particularly Mike, the floor captain, felt this. Mike didn't appreciate being slammed with multiple tables at once, and so he complained about it: "You're putting me in the weeds," he said to Richard.

After a few weeks of working with this indiscriminate management, Mike quietly approached the host station when he saw Richard leave to talk with some teenage girls dressed in miniskirts and loitering in the hotel lobby. Staged optimists are always distracted by anything that gives them attention, glory or adoration. Mike quickly grabbed a pen and added several phony names to the reservation book. While putting a small dot near the end of each name he told me, quietly in my ear, "This is quality control." When Richard returned, he saw the reservation book filled and assumed the restaurant was booked for the night.

From then on, I doctored the reservations on my own, under Mike's approving eye. It was a weird feeling of autonomy that stuck with me for life, and it came from an experience that felt like a negative action against the coercive pressure of a shortsighted boss. I was nineteen and I was running the floor.

Fake optimists do not allow others to run things on their own. It takes away from their spotlight. This is why life was great at the French restaurant until Mike took a job in Hawaii and Richard moved me to a busboy position and hired a few scantily dressed girls to run the reservation book. Richard lived in the hotel and gravitated toward new and attractive people, always taking center stage everywhere he went. He captivated new friends every few weeks, and his marriage lasted only six months. It was amazing how quickly people came and went in his life. When intimate human contact caught up with him—which happened rather fast—life became difficult as new people started to see the hollowness inside. This is why we dislike unnatural salespeople so much: they live in the world of performance and avoid walking off-stage to show who they really are. Fire them before it is too late. They are temporary energy, distractions that can cost you lasting and sustained value.

Within months, the restaurant closed, and Richard left to open another new establishment in Long Beach. Before his departure, service crumbled, experienced employees left, and a better job for me opened at a German restaurant in Santa Monica. While working with some great waiters—and learning German on the side—it took a good year to realize that the "staged optimist" is difficult to spot because we too often measure people as optimistic on a first impression. Because of the energy of the staged optimist, genuine people have become a fading flower as we stumble over charismatic liveliness as optimistic repeatedly. As long as we continue to promote the worship of a first impression, we'll never get a backstage pass to real human life.

I had a strong sense of loss when I left the French restaurant. I knew that I would miss my friendship with Mike: he was beautifully genuine amidst so much that was not. Mike offered me a first chance to *think* on the job. He also loved to talk about the meaning of things. He had a natural affection for discussion, especially one-on-one, and he inspired the best quality in others, things found only in open dialogue.

From Mike, I learned that discussion anchors the mind to all things honest and builds lasting depth needed in the art, business, government, and in our religious and family ties. Staged optimists know they have no real depth and so they avoid discussion. This is a central problem with all fake optimists.

Once you realize how staged optimists maintain a constant cheerleader performance on and off-stage, it becomes more painful working around them. They avoid showing any genuine emotional range. I'm not saying that they need to be gloomy—they just need a steady stream of honesty about who and what they are. If optimism includes honesty, then only in discussion with others can we see the real stuff we call empathy, logic, personal responsibility, patience, and friendship? Without these and more qualities, we lack real connectivity. Soon the staged optimist has nothing of value to show, and nothing of himself to offer. Not showing the real stuff when people could sure use it is being a fake optimist, the way many make a living on their performance and not on any value-added. In fact, most fake performances give the real art of acting a bad name.

The Real Art of Acting

Truly great actors use bits and pieces from their own lives to make their performances real and accessible to themselves and others. It's not just performance *on the surface*; the real stuff eventually *rises to the surface*. This translates into something believable to the audience. Skilled actors listen to other characters, and they react from their own emotional and intellectual responses. This is what is meant by the phrase "acting is believing." Orson Wells put it best when he defined the art of acting in the following way:

> There is no such thing as becoming another character by
> putting on a lot of makeup. You may need to put on the
> makeup, but what you are doing is undressing to yourself.
> And even tearing yourself apart and presenting to the
> public that part of you which corresponds to what you are
> playing. And there is a villain in each of us, a murderer
> in each of us, a fascist in each of us, a saint in each of us,
> and the actor is the man or women who can eliminate
> from himself those things which interfere with that truth.[1]

Acting is not a false notion that you *are* the character (staged optimism) but that you *believe in* the character (genuine optimism). When you truly believe in something and are willing to show it from the depths of your soul, you stand in the raw skin of who you are. You are revealing something of yourself rather than hiding behind a façade. A genuine and believable actor has enough stability in his or her own life to make the character believable to others. This exemplifies the art of true acting, to display on stage something you believe about a character on paper. It means undressing much of your real-life to show a new character from bits of yourself inside. If Hollywood truly understood the real art in acting, we would not have so much personal insecurity intruding upon the actor's performance.

Unfortunately, this is exactly the case with the staged optimist as well as many bad actors in Hollywood. They execute a strict routine without thought. They energetically telegraph their reactions and they express absolutely nothing of themselves in doing it. In the entertainment business, they're known as bad actors; in real life, they're what we call staged optimists. They are predictable and never in the moment because they're not listening to anyone—when someone is talking to them, they're preparing their next line.

You'd be surprised to learn how many well-known celebrities and politicians perform like this. Leaders in our community and at work fill the same fake role. You can tell them apart by their lack of real mental and emotional improvisational skills demanded of them in challenging theatrical scenes and in answering unscripted questions in the open public.

Fewer and fewer people take questions anymore. Too many leaders cannot improvise and move into real meaning. They were never taught improvisation, an oral tradition of constant dialogue in the home, with friends, and within one's community. They were never taught to think in concepts and to look for definition free from contradiction.

Take any person reared in an environment where he or she receives challenging questions daily and compares that person with someone who approaches learning with no connection to others. While the relational person born out of discussion is ready to lead others, the person on the lecture-and-test path struggles with leadership and a lack of vision. What is disturbing, as we will find, is that the majority of the population is subject to linear minds and not relational character. This is no fault of their own. It is just that we are mostly born into a society where a connection with others is less valued than our contact list in our phones. Would you rather talk with an author or just read her book?

Those reared on conversation try to reach a consensus. A book never questions any assumptions a reader makes in private. Therefore, what the reader concludes from reading is never tested in open discussion. Even an education based on classics that does not incorporate intensive discussion tends to promote more linear minds that learn from published authority and not personal inquiry. An education based on constant questioning and open discussion, where information does not become a matter of fact implied by some power center, is the kind of education that yields a greater relational consensus.

Look at the education of Thomas Jefferson. As a young man in his early teens, he studied under a mentor, George Wythe, along with several others. A small group of students would read great classics and show up to talk for hours about what they had read. In private they kept a commonplace book of thoughts to further build on their ability to relate the content to their own minds. There was no lecture, just an open table of discussion. Who would have thought that such an education based on a discussion of classics alone would have produced a statesman who would draft *the Declaration of Independence* and become a president of the United States? Do you think Henry David Thoreau wrote *On Civil Disobedience* without any adversarial challenge? Even Benjamin Franklin engaged in constant discussion in his private Junto group, and the famous dialogues of Socrates are derived from the pure discussion. Ralph Waldo Emerson and Thomas Carlyle conversed overseas for years via written dialogue, despite disagreement. Staged optimists are people who have never experienced this and we do not have the time to train them. So, fire them before they destroy the much-needed relational connections that generate a thriving culture in your organization.

I have a friend who challenged herself to read a book every week for a year. She accomplished this task, but not once did she engage in an open discussion about any of those books. There was no real taffy pull in testing the meaning of those books. Plus, not one of them was a classic. They were all contemporary reads of the day. We can easily debate the value of a classic, but consider that she could not recall much of what any of those books said after a few months. This is what happens when content is not allowed to sink in. I dare say that a classic can sink in because its content has that relational ability. Try it for yourself. Read the hottest self-help or personal improvement book on the market and then read Marcus Aurelius' *Meditations*. Which one will impact you the most?

Just as bad actors never receive training in the use of improvisation to reach greater range, a poor leader lacks the experience of confrontation and taking questions in the open. Just reading a book doesn't mean we are able to question its conclusions. Once, I purchased a used copy of a groundbreaking book that won the Pulitzer Prize for general nonfiction. A previous reader had marked it up, and every written comment showed this reader's ignorance. Had others been there during the reading, they could have questioned the bad conclusions written in the margin. Fake and often linear minds never engage in a confrontation that challenges their own minds, so they lack the relational skill found in the genuine optimism that I'm referring to in this book, the kind that lives by intimate human interaction. If we continue to believe a book alone is richer in content than a conversation with living human beings about that book, we will continue to reject each other's agency as a value in our lives. Superiority and elitism will continue to separate those with a deep reading list from those with honest questions to ask.

The author Samuel Louis Dael has an incredible reach into religious studies, psychology, physics, epistemology, and philosophy. His writings are derived from keeping a question alive through generations of discussion in his own family and from friends and lay colleagues. Compare that to the average scholar today who derives his or her work from countless published works and from the most recent peer-reviewed articles. Where is the open challenge from all walks of life and over a long period of time? No wonder innovation is stifled in academia. No wonder academia has lost its will to engage honest questions from genuine concern. Referencing the most recent dated study is more valued than contextual understanding.

Camera angles, editing, loud music and hidden teleprompters with adjusted lighting all mask a lack of depth and understanding. In the fake arena of life, the staged optimist avoids real discussion and never enters the open forum of dissent against his own authority unless it is on safe turf of their choosing. The bigger the audience with a popular focus, the less they need to show anything real and genuine. I find it interesting that modern Democrats and even some Republicans rarely take honest questions from opposing perspectives. John F Kennedy and Reagan were never like that. They were equally comfortable taking questions from all political perspectives. It is as though we have learned to self-corner our minds to maintain a fake impression of openness.

Staged optimists have learned exactly how to perform without believing in anything that can be openly questioned. This explains the rise of so many politicians who rhetorically speak as passionate leaders without the will to engage in open discussion. They perform without letting others challenge any belief. As Orson Wells said, they refuse to show that special truth to which they "subscribe their entire soul."

Achilles Heel

Staged optimists don't like to sit around and talk about the meaning of things. This is their Achilles heel. Too much open discussion reveals their internal emptiness, which is why they live for the public stage—removed from the proximity of prying eyes. However, with enough open and intimate talk (face-to-face if possible), and certainly over time, they reveal their true nature. It always takes time to spot them, and herein lies the rub.

For example, a handyman arrived at my house. When he entered, he was full of energy and quick to talk up a storm. This is the best way to spot staged optimists: they talk themselves up as the main attraction with know-it-all insights on every subject. Hired to do sheet-rock and finish carpentry, this handyman surprised us by behaving lewdly toward my wife. He had nothing of value that he truly believed with his whole heart; he was an empty pervert and a dead giveaway as a staged optimist. His perverted over-confidence didn't keep him on the job. It got him fired. Back then, it took two days for me to recognize the situation. Now it's immediate. As we age and learn, we become faster at reading fake optimists.

It would be great if we could apply the same real-time scrutiny to public figures and leaders in all walks of life. If they could sit in our living rooms or in a local neighborhood forum, and if we could listen to their responses to questions and comments taught by our parents, our spouses, even our children, and neighbors, then certainly everything would surface—and teleprompter-free! Talk-show hosts have lost this art of honest questioning, and reporters no longer have an independent voice that seeks clear answers. For this and many other reasons, people accept the idea that the outward projection of self-confidence is optimism. Without having to reveal what they truly believe, these fake minds exemplify the staged optimist. The time has come to fire them.

Because we all love confidence and smiles, we're easily seduced by every new performance that comes along. Unfortunately, most of us cannot see genuine people until we can get them to talk about real things. This is how we find motive and meaning in human character: we engage in open discussion without a controlling figure telling us what and how to think. A relational context reveals those people who do not operate inside one.

We must prefer open inquiry to executive control. By not requiring free expression to inquire around public expressions of meaning, staged optimists get to hide their motives behind the executive desk. Today it is even worse, they are media pundits hiding behind agendas funded by interlocking corporate directorships. We can change this by demanding more discussion and by slowing the process and by allowing the individual expression of dissent. It's the only way to make thoughtful reflection work. The first Lincoln Douglass Debates between Abraham Lincoln and Stephen A. Douglass were conducted in many locations. The format for each debate started with one candidate speaking for 60 minutes, followed by the other candidate speaking for 90 minutes, and then the first candidate was allowed a 30-minute "rejoinder." The debates were later published in their long format in the local papers for readers to follow.

Today, too many political people, celebrities, mid-level managers, and executives and leaders in many positions are not thoughtful at all, which is why we need to fire them. They are not equipped to handle the long-format discussion and they cannot stand to hear disagreement. We need a better model of human organization that allows for equal footing for considerate and relational minds. We will soon find that discussion organized by a greater degree of social discourse will keep fake optimists from exercising deflection that eventually inhibits the progress of a thriving culture.

The Use of Deflection

Staged optimists do not like to talk about the meaning of things. They live for the public stage, removed from any questioning. It takes skill to spot them, and the only way to see them is to understand how they deflect answering questions.

Staged optimists fight against dissenting voices, while genuine optimists listen deliberately to find additional facts. Staged optimists move the conversation to politically correct terminology to intimidate any dissent. They sometimes apply defensible indifference when the conversation gets a little too thick in real meaning, and they avoid a personally invested conviction by pulling a gag. You can see this when they deflect their lack of depth by politely walking their audience through rude laughter. We think they are smart and witty when the intent is to draw the attention back to them. Take a moment and view old late-night talk show hosts like Johnny Carson, Jack Par, and others and compare them to the late-night hosts today. There was a time when the guest was the center of attention, even if it meant the host had to debase himself. Today, the host is everything, and real information about the guest is held back. The mastery of deflection keeps others from seeing a lack of understanding.

As John Stewart Mill said, "The silencing of discussion is an assumption of infallibility."[2] The discussion has to come out of the agreement and not out of assumed authority.

Staged optimists deflect dissenting voices that might help reach an agreement. It will always be easier to spot someone shutting down dissent than it will be to follow the money or see a bad decision, so it's an easy clue to spot those people to fire.

We never know the silent intent of the staged optimist serving some power center behind the scenes. Even the best of us fall into the trap of following some authority because we have learned the skill of deflecting away any responsibility to question them. When England imposed a stamp act on all manufactured products and textiles made in America before the Revolution, the real motive was to limit the industrial power America was gaining over England. The use of the tax in America and not equally applied in England deflected attention away from that political truth.

So what did the colonists do in response? Did they attack the industrialists in England working behind the scenes to shut down America, or did the colonists shut down their idolatry for a king? They went after the king. By shutting down the king, they shut down the unjust tax. Read *The Declaration of Independence* and note how it lists abuses by the King that were done to maintain central control—all to bolster the wealthy in England.

Most of the time, fake optimists use deflection as part of an argument for some good, but this implied good simply means more control. The staged optimist says, "Give me all the power, the honor, and the money, and I'll show what great works I can do." We only hear brief clips of these staged optimists' speeches, and there's often little honesty in them. If these unquestioned promoters organized a small discussion in which everyone had an equal opportunity to speak, we would come to know the truth faster through more open inquiry than what we get through mass media's subliminal narrative.

Staged optimists truly hate questions from an opponent. This is why seemingly optimistic narratives hide behind controlled presentations written for our supposed good. When these false optimists make fantastic statements such as, "We must save the earth," the statement covers their real motive, and all we see are the deflective words encouraging us to trust them.

Deflecting the issue with a fantastic statement shows how a staged optimist can avoid any confrontation that might reveal some underlying motive, such as a new carbon tax scheme they are personally invested in. They hide behind optimistic statements thanks to the word associations employed. We cannot debate *must, save,* and *earth,* because ideas that are desirable deflect the mind from the truth—in this case, the desire for control over the world's natural resources.

"Everyone has a right to affordable health care" is another optimistic deflection. *Everyone, right,* and *health* again deflect us from the motive of large insurance corporations desirous of gaining control over every healthcare transaction. By limiting the competition you control the market.

At one time, we broke up monopolies with anti-trust legislation. However, when they have become ignored and commonplace, we lost control by empowering corporate control. Free enterprise and natural competition no longer survive. All that we have left are bloated governments and bloated corporations that have lost their heart to stand against powers that have grown greater than their own.

It was no surprise to see President Obama employ that same rhetoric when speaking of his healthcare act when he said the debate "is and should be over."[3] This is odd since there never was a debate. When you have one side of the political aisle vote for a bill, and the other side votes unanimously against the same bill, this isn't a debate. A lack of consensus is a direct lack of real freedom in a discussion. A majority vote is not consensus when it fails to hear dissent.

A classic deflection was the *fat-free diet,* which has an additional component: deflection by association. For many years, food processors had trouble preserving the shelf life of processed foods. Ever since pasteurization and homogenization became the norm in dairy products, larger corporations sought to eliminate fat from foods to extend the shelf life. A medical doctor came along at the perfect time and said, "Fat causes heart disease." This was a perfect deflection, allowing marketing campaigns to remove fats from products, increase the shelf-life, and sell the by-product to animal feed producers (or have more fats, like butter, to sell). Since then we've learned that pasteurization kills enzymes, making milk an allergic product for many people. Most recently, even heart specialists have stated that Omega 3 fatty acids can help heart patients. We now have the common knowledge of good fats versus bad fats. Despite this, the public mind still thinks consuming fat equals a fat tummy.

We will not see the truth for many years because of our lust for cheap, highly processed foods. Few people understand the body's ability to convert empty calories into fatty tissue. Statistically, weight gain has increased substantially since fat-free starches and sugars have become the new staple. This isn't a conspiracy: it's the central control model of linear thinking that moves food processing away from smaller communities to larger processing plants. Improved transportation has also centralized production and empowered massive corporations, subliminal mass media, and more government control.

The problem is that the community is falling apart because it has lost all culture for conversation. National advertisers have replaced local dialogue, and gossip is a social network post. If you are a person who follows a lot of alternative media and from many different sources, just try to strike up a conversation with those who still get their information from one or two mainstream outlets. It is fast becoming clear that we're losing touch with our neighbors. The whole world has become a virtual landscape of fake optimism.

Point of No Return

We've come to the point of no return because we think, "authority knows best" rather than allowing "free and open discussion to decide." The first is linear and centralizes all responsibility; the latter is relational and decentralizes responsibility. We no longer have to see, learn, and understand as long as a doctor in a white lab coat does it for us.

Silencing discussion and dissent, in time, becomes the default mission of staged authority. We are fast becoming a generation that learns to hide our minds—a fundamental trait of staged optimism.

Notice the traits of Staged Optimists to the right aligned with characteristics to the left. When combined, we call each a *character trait*. When it comes to the character trait of idolatry, staged optimists are driven by glory. They demand the reward of attention and their intelligence is defined by social position and not by their ideas or their value-added. Each fake optimist we will discuss shows his character through unique traits. We will apply the same characteristics to all fake optimists; however, their traits are different. When we apply the same characteristics to genuine optimists, a unique distinction will surface with entirely different traits. The only change is with the character of *faith,* which better describes the traits of genuine optimists while *idolatry* describes fake optimists. Here are the character traits of a staged optimist. If you see these character traits in people, fire them as soon as you can. They will eventually destroy the entire organization. See **Figure 1-1**

Fig. 1–1 Traits of the Staged Optimist

Character	Traites
Idolatry	Seeks Control
Intelligence	Glory in Position
Agency	Disobeys Truth
Motivation	Desires Honor
Reward	Demads Attention

Bigotry and discrimination have inspired many people to get involved in civil rights. Over time we've chosen to accept a new direction of incremental centralization of control in business, government, and in community organizations. Built to mask the hidden intent, fake optimists call themselves progressives to deflect from their controlling agenda. Odd as it may seem, the word progressive is often just another form of force. Through national government force or a politically correct policy in an organization, we trade our local freedom for some demanding social justice at a distance said to be progressive. Constitutions may guarantee civil liberties (the right to life, liberty, and privacy), but not a personal right to take from the government. Today there is more interest in demanding more personal rights than in an effort to preserve civil liberties for all. This has to do with the linear thinking of fake optimists. Let me give an example.

Imagine a wealthy community with higher property tax revenue to support their education and imagine a poor community not having enough revenue for education. The statist progressive will seek to equalize funds between communities. With this approach, both communities lose consent in how they educate. The progressive equalizer of all things never looks at equality of rights between individuals in a community, which is what a constitution protects, but instead, the progressive wants to solve the inequality between communities and even whole groups, and all in the name of being progressive, which carries with it a false optimism. All you have to do is call yourself a progressive and you stand on moral ground free from debate and dissent against that stand. Those who dare question are automatically negative, racist, xenophobic and on and on.

Today, the progressive who wants to force equality across the board now wants global equality with absolutely no local consent. So, in the name of doing good to claim a fake optimistic end, power is centralized, which is the opposite of genuine voice. And when you centralize power, you distance the freedom to dissent against that power. Progressives rarely consider the unintended consequences when they centralize authority and power in the name of universal equality. They are fake optimists pushing a totalitarian end. They are the perfect examples of being staged, always for a universal good (the big theater) but never for a local voice (natural improvisation).

Only in preserving civil liberties first can we promote personal and social responsibility in the community rather than support more global force at greater distances. The key is *in the community.* This is the optimal place for genuine optimism to flourish and the only way to reach the greatest level of diversity the world has ever seen. Why? Because it is the only place where conversation and discussion can openly function to reach a greater level of social consent. Centralize consent in just a few hands outside the community and we become an authoritarian society. The community then dies and the culture that binds us diminishes. This is much of America today and everyone who is pushing more progressive solutions over local innovation should be fired.

When we conserve as much social responsibility as possible at a local level, then the fake-progressive no longer has an excuse for taking responsibility away. When will conservatives, libertarians, and constitutionalists ever figure this out? As long as they refuse to scale the consent of one person into the consent of a local community, they will never combat controlling oligarchs from usurping control of local responsibility for personal gain. It is time we get away from the constitution as a "cure-all." It is not a living exercise of responsibility; it only protects against the abuse of individual liberties for a short while until the new progressive idolatry rewrites it.

If conservatives would start talking of community sustainability and even use phrases like "local community," "sovereign culture," or "neighborhood consent," this would easily rob the controlling minds on both sides of the political aisle that push for national socialism controlled by executive orders and federal bureaucracies. Hey, why not even take the phrase "community socialism," have it run by a micro republic of direct and unanimous consent, and just watch the federal oligarchs squirm at losing their central control. If not that, then use the phrase "community capitalism." Again, the relational mind (the genuine) that decentralizes power and widens consent within local and modular bodies needs to confront the linear mind (the fake) that centralizes power and narrows access in giving consent.

Oddly, controlling statists fail to see how more control or centralized authority does not demand any more responsibility from the individual or the community. In fact, it is just the opposite. Controlling minds pushing for centralized control seldom understand this. They advocate that the state take control of social responsibilities to remove their guilt for not showing any responsibility on their own. List ten politicians and compare them with a local cooperative business venture. Add up all the money, service, and value-added to the community by each and you'll quickly see the selfishness of political elitists and the true service of the local cooperative.

If all responsibility for social good is controlled at the national or even state level, or even at the highest level of a corporation, then laws and policy are written without local consent. This is fake and destructive. Even worse, we do this without any room to invest in our own liberty. Always remember that liberty is what adds value. Give this liberty to controllers at great distances and you'll lose your voice in the process and all invested responsibility in your community. Optimism to add value locally is then removed. We call this plantation politics. Let the people vote themselves largess from the public treasury, manage what you give them with a large bureaucratic machine, and watch the people become dependent and not liberated. Watch them care less for their neighbor and no longer cleave one to another.

When civil rights become more important than personal responsibility, we foster the plan of tyrants and not the plan of the people under God. It is through personal responsibility scaled into the community and the organized culture of consent that we preserve civil rights. We should always work to inspire the taking of more responsibility locally and not giving it away. Progressive minds and even social justice advocates want to take social responsibility away from people. This only kills the enthusiasm in each person within the community to add value.

Changing the meaning of a term to obtain more central control and deflect away from local responsibility is a staged optimist's way of avoiding the truth. It's the fundamental cause of darkness throughout history. Darkness covered the true meaning of Christianity when the early saints ceded power to Roman authority. Even after a long Reformation that brought us out of this darkness, Hitler, Mao, Stalin, and others from the last century saw fit to alter the right to bear arms in order to obtain complete control—all in the name of safety and protection—false intentions for wicked ends.

If we take away responsibility, we are already dead. And if we choose to empower controlling authority at a great distance to replace the work of a local community, we will continue to slide down the path of annihilation. Fire staged optimists. They are in a constant battle against the true spirit of freedom that takes responsibility individually and conserves it locally.

All-Energy, No Spark

Talk with staged optimists about the definition of reason, about the meaning of education, intelligence, or love. Ask them questions about vision—and you'll quickly see their lack of it. You may find that staged optimists voice opinions about physical exercise, food, and cars, and even express minor emotions about human relations, and sometimes you'll hear instead a trivial political talking-point used to sound informed. What you won't find is the insight that defines a deliberate life that adds value. You may find a cordial smile and great oral delivery, but not the willingness to stand and hear disagreement.

It is time we all study collective meritocracies. They are the positioning of a growing body that advances people through adulation engineering. This is the process of honoring a power above to gain or secure a position below. Together, this collective authority approves people for advancement in such a way as to maintain a central and vertical power structure. This is how controllers dressed in staged optimism work.

While the merit of an independent mind may choose to rise on its own, a fake person is always looking for the power center or central power group with which to align. This is why majority-rule organizations are so destructive. Political staging of artificial optimism never succeeds by showing an independent thought publicly, but rather it comes from the praise of a power center in an idolized and worshipped majority. We see over and over how idolatry, without faith, drives fake optimists.

This is why we lack honesty in open discussion. Our expressions are controlled in a centrally manipulated collective, which requires our adoration for authority under the false impression that we are working as a team. Open disagreement is completely removed, and this is witnessed across corporate, religious and government structures.

Plato's *Republic* is a good example. He fabricated a collective hierarchy designed to cover the collective intent of control. Socrates, on the other hand, didn't aspire to create a vertical power structure to stage collective control. He preferred open discussion in order to encourage honest meaning from each individual. Socrates never sought central control: education came from small discussions rather than national mandates.

Again, always look at how we idolize authority and centralize control. It's much easier to determine political corruption than by trying to follow the money.

Political structures in business create a collective that's often designed to cover self-seeking motives. Each person, engulfed in a collective hierarchy who doesn't allow individual dissent, is left intimidated. Some people appeal to certain controlling figures to get their acceptance, while others are willing to stand to correct collective power. Only the latter is genuinely optimistic, even though this person appears the most antagonistic in the collective.

But there's a catch. Optimism through dissent must also be willing to stand correction. Just putting the dissenter in power doesn't guarantee the next dissenter the same freedom. We cannot say, "question everything" and then not "stand to be corrected." This second half of the principle doesn't survive well from one generation to another. When anyone tries to surface a nonconforming view, collective controllers deflect the attempt by saying, "We're off-subject," or "we need to get with the program." The dissenters then appear anti-optimistic. Shutting them down is not an act of responsibility.

When run entirely by a central authority, the collective organization, whether a church, a political party, or a business meeting, has its own staged optimists ready to walk away from questioning minds. As a principle, whole groups, when managed in this way, rarely act responsibly. Suffice it to say that staged optimists thrive on very large collective structures that allow them to take center stage without revealing the center of their hearts. Fire them.

Staged optimists avoid all forms of open expression that may reveal their lack of understanding. In every situation, they rarely say what they believe. The only way to find any spark of understanding in them is when the staged optimist is open and free to take questions. How many times have you listened to a speaker or leader and wanted to ask a direct question? Because you weren't able to submit your question, the leader wasn't challenged or doubted.

Something is wrong when the values of an entire generation favor diversity of opinion over an open discussion. Diversity allows for meaning to remain in a constant state of relativity, whereas open discussion flushes the true meaning out. Discussion guarantees diversity, but diversity itself does not always guarantee discussion. Fake optimists hide behind diversity. Genuine optimists ask for more discussion.

What would happen with Alcoholics Anonymous if a lecturer replaced group discussion? Nobody would receive correction in front of those who have learned to read a staged act. Group therapy dies under the lecture format. We are likewise dead in a society that shuts down dissent out of some form of positive political tolerance designed to control the group.

Colleges and universities teach the importance of cultural diversity, yet we never hear anyone talking about open discussion. To have any cultural value, it's imperative that we maintain the freedom to dissent from every so-called authority in a specific culture and be willing to receive correction ourselves. For instance, a willingness to stand correction is better than cultural diversity. John Locke talked about this in his "Letter Concerning Toleration" in 1689. Toleration opens a hearing for discussion; cultural diversity does not.

Unfortunately, much of the power academia has over fake optimism takes dissent as antagonistic to diversity. Diversity is a political form of fake optimism designed to make truth relative. This is seen when various selected ideas are given equal expression but none are challenged. It is like the perpetual Israel and Palestine conflict. If you question Israel, you are an anti-Semite. If you question Palestine, you are an imperial Zionist. Therefore, no questions are allowed otherwise we might trigger people into sudden war.

It is like kicking Socrates out of the city for asking too many questions about the meaning of things and letting Plato stay because he appeals to collective diversity with the same self-interest. Plato was linear and a staged optimist. Socrates was relational, genuine, and willing to die for it. For good reason, Samuel Dael calls Plato's *Republic* "a manual for despots and a bible for dictators."[4] Plato's *Republic* was never the foundation of western civilization. The dialogues of Socrates were. While Plato's *Republic* is the source text for all control freaks, the source text of a free society is constant discussion or free voluntary association with no compulsion.

Why we've allowed Plato to remain the central focus of western tradition is a complete mystery. Just look at how we continue designing society around controlling authority (Plato's King model) but never do we look to promote common consent in modular form (a genuine Socratic process) supported by independent and free minds.

All collective meritocracies build on the central control of a select few intellectuals who self-select through peer authorities and adulation engineering. They build a central and vertical power structure to stage their optimism and avoid horizontal discussions to determine the meaning of things that actually might expose the politics of their falsified optimism.

Group therapy comes from the premise that the socially sick are hiding something they cannot face alone. This only works in a headless body where every person in the small group is equal in the group and the group needs to be small. The idea is to transform a staged lie to genuine optimism because the staged person is mentally ill. Mental patients are intellectually skilled at deflection. Open discussion, over time, is the only method for healing them. This does not imply what the best content for discussion should be. It just says that even the mentally sick have the freedom to question others who are mentally sick, including the doctor. Read *One Flew Over a Cuckoo's Nest* by Ken Kesey. An international bestseller in the 1960s and later won five academy awards for the film. Such a piece of literature with wide appeal deserves more importance than the newest academic research study ready to promote the newest syndrome.

Open discussion from all participants is the only way to see true motive and fake optimism. When we hear others raise questions we never considered, we are all enlightened. At its core, social responsibility provides for the talk that is more open and less centralized in control. Such a superior method of autonomous discussion brings about greater freedom and more responsibility held in common by the people rather than idolatrous authority or agenda mob over them.

A good example is my local water conservancy district with a small board of directors that self-selects itself and controls everything. I have wanted to get involved due to the ideas I have of using twin oxide instead of fluoride to clean and purify water. Is it easy for me to add value found from my research? No! Is there any open-door for me to get involved and add my voice? No! The water conservancy board is like 99% of all orga-nizations; it is a political structure not inherently open to new ideas below its ranks. If 320 people in the community sudden-ly wanted to get involved, and if twelve people in that group had ideas and systems they would like to see implemented, how would the leadership know about these ideas? They don't be-cause there is no system in play to give that number of people that kind of access to such a limited power structure. We never think to enlarge and widen access.

I am not talking about another suggestion box. I am talking about real social inclusion. We do not see how to do this, so we quickly conclude it is impossible. Maybe we should define a few terms, as this book intends to do so that we can help others see the possibility, then maybe more of us can see the problem and why fake optimists have gotten control of so much of our lives.

Definition Par Excellence

When it comes to revealing fake optimists of all types, especially the staged optimist, the battleground is in the mean-ing of words. The challenge is to acquire an independent and re-sponsible meaning of words like logic, liberty, mercy, freedom, love, and friendship. The meaning we give these words is what drives us. By revealing our meaning, we disclose our motive through everything we do. Staged optimists do not reveal their motives because they have very little meaning.

Even more, many abstract words like these become our character. Fake optimists do not assign consistent meaning to words. More often, they change the meanings of words by im-plying a new set of terms to replace the old. If we know the old definition and if we see a new meaning emerging, we can see the person's inner motive. If we could, we would see that the new term is truly false. That's the point. Attaching responsi-ble meaning to key abstract words is what gives real strength to stand against the staged optimist. It's so important that Marcus Aurelius wrote the following in his *Meditations*:

Remember how long you have been putting off these things, and how often you have received an opportunity from the gods, and yet do not use it. You must now at last perceive of what universe you are a part and from what administrator of the universe your existence flows, and that a limit of time is fixed for you, which if you do not use for clearing away the clouds from your mind, it will go and you will go, and it will never return.[5]

When we refuse to clear away the clouds from our minds regarding the meaning of important words in open discourse, we are subjected to the meanings that authorities feed us. Too often, these meanings include neither real value nor responsible action. Even worse, when forced upon us without our consent and without the ability to object, we begin to accept the new definitions without relational understanding.

At the end of talking about the three fake optimists, we need to fire, you can find an addendum that gives a list of the most challenging words to define. Defining these words in the context of responsibility (as opposed to the context of control) is the substance of meaning that gives belief real strength. The only way to find the responsible meaning is to engage in the practice of reaching consent. In other words, we all need to define these words in relation to long format discussion so we can stand against all fake optimists who alter meanings for narrow intentions.

The real meaning we hold about words makes up our personal beliefs, written laws, and social and business policy. The greatest leaders define their words within the context of open and public consent. If the world of modern physics would engage in an open discussion with etymologists, epistemologists and even historians about the meaning of space or time, they could no longer pontificate their ideas fueled by a desire for magic.

If we never define important terms in the open and in the face of possible dissent, we're more apt to accept a new definition by a charismatic authority over a wide spectrum of agreement. When this happens, we give our responsibility to hear dissent over to some centralized authority.

All you have to do is see how staged personalities respond to your real mind and when you take responsibility for what you truly believe. And what genuine optimists believe is seen in the open, when they willingly define and live their definitions in the face of open dissent.

Great actors come out from behind their fear and are open about what they're willing to take responsibility for and what they believe. Bad actors don't listen to others on stage, and when they do pretend to listen and share the stage, you can see in their eyes their impatience and a quick return to their canned delivery in order to take back the stage. Staged optimists do not read what you believe, and they certainly do not want to hear it. They appeal to the collective hierarchy and avoid responding to you. They service narcissism and not one's real need.

When I was in graduate school, there was a professor who was having inappropriate relationships with his female students. Everyone thought he was suffering from childhood problems, identity issues that he couldn't resolve, which led to his decision to divorce his wife. I was armed with insights from Shakespeare, Ernest Becker, and Otto Rank, plus countless years of discussion with my father about human motive, including several years as a voyeur bartender, but my open disagreement made me an outcast at a social gathering of academics and my fellow students when I dared say, "he has no childhood issues, he's just afraid of death."

The need to complicate behavior with trendy excuses or experiences in the far distant youth exhibits something staged optimists do. It allows them to blame their parents, their culture or the indeterminate past while hiding the fear within. It's a powerful form of deflection. It allows the staged person to hide the root motive, which was my argument, and avoid the responsibility needed to accept it.

Fire the Staged Optimist

The false face we paint for ourselves to get through the maze of the day represses the fear we refuse to accept. We get others to follow us who seek the same escape. When the staged optimist does this, the deception becomes especially difficult to read: we are all attracted to an unaffected person who's able to lie without remorse. While the fake person moves along unaffected, the genuine person stumbles and her stammering shows a person trying to reveal more honesty. Fire the first person and hire the second.

Imagine a young man struggling to ask a girl out for the first time. At that moment, he is most real and genuine because his fear has risen to the surface. Genuine optimists are responsible; they reveal their true heart and mind to the world. If you think they're prideful, consider that they've learned that as soon as they volunteer too much, others complain. Take a job in a labor union shop, work harder and give more in service to others, and watch the reaction of complaints against your hard work making others look bad. Walk into a social or religious function with a willingness to serve with modesty and kindness and you'll sometimes get similar results. Sustain the status quo of every power center or the collective hierarchy, on the other hand, and you'll receive the love desired.

The time for a new cultural model is approaching, as every interaction increasingly ends in more central control, which comes from the easy political manipulation of majority rule. This is where we find a kind of upbeat intimidation feeding on the power of a central-control grid.

We can now see. Staged optimists follow trends rather than any developed insight within themselves. They pretend to have a life full of vitality, but in no way express a vision of value. They remain stuck with common and clichéd verbiage derived from acceptable fashion and not responsible focus. They demonstrate smooth language, but they keep from answering questions by taking upon themselves the central entertainment fixture. While at center stage, they deflect criticism by being obtuse just to give a poise of confidence. They maintain a rock star presence but it's the same old executive distance.

In public, we want unaffected souls and upbeat happiness, and we thrive on false modesty rather than on genuine goodness. Think about it. We counsel depressed people or those struggling through life to justify our unwillingness to understand and serve them. If people honestly express dissent, the fake optimist says to them, "You need to be a little political." Can we build great companies, cultures, and communities on being political and fake? No!

We want happy faces to hide the struggles going on inside. This is why we are attracted to so many staged optimists. If not this, we tend to desire a different kind of optimism, a second type of fake optimism that exists under a different guise, a guise more pernicious and even more difficult to spot. It is the fraudulent optimism of the *intimidator*.

2
The Intimidating Optimist

We all tend to alter the meaning of words to justify our worldview. One might feel guilty or jealous for any reason, but rather than accept the guilt, we change the meaning of words to curb our regret. If we do not alter the meaning of words to deflect their imposition on us, we simply avoid talking about them or we shut down all access to any peer review.

Samuel Louis Dael

Intimidation

On February 4, 2005, while promoting social security reform in Omaha, Nebraska, President George W. Bush stepped into an unscripted moment and spoke with Mary Monin, a divorced woman in her fifties and a mother of three children, one of whom was a mentally challenged son. Here is a short excerpt of that dialogue:[1]

President Bush: "...there is a certain comfort to know that the promises made will be kept by the government. You don't have to worry."

Without prompting, Ms. Monin responded, "That's good because I work three jobs and I feel like I contribute."

The President: "You work three jobs?"

Ms. Monin: "Three jobs, yes."

The President replied: "Uniquely American, isn't it? I mean, that is fantastic that you're doing that." The audience then broke into applause and the president followed with "Get any sleep?"

President Bush could have said, "It's difficult when single parents are left alone in these dire conditions." This would have stated the problem. The president could have followed with, "I will have someone contact you because I want to learn more." This shows concern, but with no obligation. The public already knows that this fundamental problem exists and it would be better to have someone local follow through specifically. Instead, he chose to say, "That is fantastic."

Intimidator optimists avoid a follow-up that even a local volunteer could handle and report back on. At any rate, President Bush could have seized a great opportunity to say something like, "This kind of hardship comes from too much Washington control and not enough local autonomy to help one another. We need more community care and less government largess. It is time Americans cleave to one another again." Rather than stand up and say something powerful, he used his one-liner to distract people from his lack of leadership while the audience responded in full applause. This is the fake optimism of the intimidator, completely void of any responsible faith.

We call this intimidator optimism because it sounds enthusiastic in speech. Unfortunately buried in the words is a kind of positive mental exertion imposed on your own free will. For example, is it "uniquely American" (meaning a good thing) to work three jobs and raise three children alone as a single parent? Where is the hope for something better in that claim? It is not genuinely optimistic. It's fake.

Fake optimists avoid responsibility by dismissing important human relationships with a deflective gag, and a lot of people laugh along, escaping in turn from being humanly connected. The modern self-help and positive-attitude movements promote this kind of dismissive attitude toward those truly going through tough times. Because life does have trials, one's attitude is not always positive on the surface, and yet the intimidator optimist is quick to impose guilt for not being upbeat. This is especially true when you express doubts about certain decisions or doubts about ideas by offering better decisions and better ideas.

Even with the friendliest of attitudes, better decisions and better ideas promote the same reactionary distaste from intimidator optimists, and they will label you as negative simply to create distance.

While staged optimists avoid open discussion; intimidator optimists shut it down. This is how they create distance. Intimidator optimists are easy to spot because they never show any real encouragement that leaves a person's agency fully in place: they're strictly linear in their stand-alone thinking rather than relational in connecting with others. And they will shut others down from expressing a potentially better way that more of us can relate to.

Intimidators hate better ways. Better ways force them to see a wider field and to assume some responsibility for a new direction. It is as though they have an innovation threshold, and they alone maintain the line and keep others from crossing that threshold.

A better way to understand is that the intimidator hates to think in relational contexts. They use emergency actions with new goal-setting to distract us from new ideas. They even make peripheral issues of protocol, procedure, and planning the new central vision. This is sure to shut down effective insights and advance only those who are the fakest or the most political.

Every generation has its ways of intimidating others to maintain control to preserve their views. Look at *The Power of Positive Thinking* (1952). It came at a time when people were losing religious faith. And because nature abhors a vacuum, writers were trying to replace faith with something else. What we failed to see is that we'd misused faith in the first place by giving too much of its interpretation to religious authority. Some years later, we got *How to Cure Yourself of Positive Thinking* (1977), which had some popularity, but quickly we put it aside in favor of new upbeat happiness under pressure, a kind of forced thinking and the many ideas of cognitive attraction that followed. We were then told, "you are what you think." This led to, "change your thinking and you will be more positive."

It is as if we have rejected a fanatic faith in favor of a fanatic optimism. Never did we think to define false optimism as we should have defined a controlled religious faith. Society falls into darkness when it starts to define words like *faith* in terms of magic and not in terms of *responsible action*.

Let's Define

Let's define intimidation and faith with a very simple approach. If words like love, justice, and even liberty imply some kind of responsible action—without saying what that action is—then surely faith requires a responsible action of its own. However, with the word intimidation, the idea of responsible action is not implied. Instead, we see a force applied to our agency. With faith, there is no force. With intimidation, there is no freedom to act responsibly.

If we say, "faith is irrational," then we reject a better definition that might say, "faith is responsible."

There's a kind of fake optimism that is coerced. We call this intimidation; it represents a complete absence of any responsible action that we might simply call faith.

Imagine a boss telling an employee that a cut in hours will require moving his employee from the night shift to the early-morning shift. The boss knows the employee took the job because it fit with his afternoon classes at the local college. This boss also knows that the employee's wife works the early-morning hours at the county hospital and that every morning his employee takes care of two boys to get them off to school. With hands up to excuse himself and shrugging his shoulders, the boss says, "Life is ten percent what you make it, and ninety percent how you take it."

Because the employee does not take change with a smile, his expressed doubt becomes *his* problem.

Intimidating optimism forces consent while avoiding any real concerned connection. This is how linear thinkers behave: their approach is cold, but—from their point of view—

always upbeat. I use the word linear to explain fake optimists because thinking in a very narrow and confined way with no peripheral insight from others is a philosophy sold by countless self-improvement books and a fundamental approach used by the growing coaching industry. Let me ask you a question. Are you tired of self-improvement with no real social or cultural improvement? Then so are the many beginning to see the truth about optimism being coopted by personal self-interest. It's not our attitudes but how we organize as a people that best defines optimism.

If we repress the voice or self-expression of anyone, we have a problem with promoting the fakest among us. But if we work to organize in a way that hears the voice of everyone, we have a thriving culture.

Masked by controlled executive decision-making and delivering their messages with the appeal of smooth oratory, intimidating optimists avoid any personal responsibility in their relations with others. This is why they are terrible leaders and why we should fire them.

That boss *could* have said, "I'm sorry, but because of budget cuts, I had to adjust everyone's hours. Others have similar problems and I need some temporary rotation so all can make the best of a bad situation."

The difference between intimidation and encouragement is significant. Command-and-control intimidation does a lot of damage to human encouragement because it demands automatic assimilation to cow-tow, appease, and pander to power. Dissenting innovation or simple disagreement are not invited. It's high time we saw the difference between a linear path of intimidation and a relational path of encouragement. This book is that paradigm shift.

It's one thing deliberately to control a business meeting to avoid being bogged down in a round-table complaint session. It's another to shut down a work-through discussion for the sake of expediency and without an honest field of consent. Intimidation then becomes an imposition on developing a genuine concern for ideas and questions that others have. We can tend to intimidate constant complaining, and sometimes this is needed to build a stronger spine, but at the same time what do we do with those with honest questions and real ideas? Surfacing these already shows a spine and intimidator optimists are known to shut them out.

The Vast Problem

A good friend nearing retirement from her position at a local college suddenly came face-to-face with the demands of saying yes when saying no stood in line with the logic of her heart and her years of valuable experience. The culprit was an intimidator optimist. He was the new vice-president of student services, a pureblood "yes" enforcer. He wanted to eliminate a vital scholarship program and put more money into marketing, to attract more students to the college. He was reaching for greater enrollment numbers versus bringing the best students to the school. He didn't realize that by reaching for the best students through scholarship offerings, other students would follow, and enrollment would naturally increase: a college is only as great as the students it attracts.

Nonetheless, he approached my friend and asked her to help him; his unstated implication was, "get on board or quit." He went even further, telling all of his staff, "If you don't like your job, find a way to like it. And if you can't find a way to like it, find another job." Everyone just nodded in forced affirmation while a few said "no!" in solemn soliloquy.

Here's the problem. Non-political people can't hide their disagreement, and the yes enforcer quickly sees who they are: so it makes sense to express the feelings openly anyway because the enforcer won't be fooled by anything else. So what did my friend do? She voiced her mind and retired early and left the college.

At the time, there was just no way to stand against this new VP because of his commanding upbeat tone. Any attempt to question him would come off looking professionally negative rather than expressing a need to ask for honest clarity.

In the corporate world, questioning minds aren't considered team players. If you aren't a team player, you are a negative person. What if corporate models suddenly chose to let doubt and new ideas arise? The only way it could happen would be inside a new model of horizontal consent.

To understand the vast problem of fake optimism in the form of positive intimidation, imagine the testing of a twelve-year-old's adoption into a violent gang. The older gang leader tells the new recruit to rob the home of a retired couple on his street to be initiated. Once the kid starts to show a little hesitation, the gang leader immediately says in front of everyone in the brotherhood, "We're your family. Do this for your brothers."

How could a twelve-year-old stand up against that? Yet take any positive one-liner out of any self-help book—and the young boy would still find himself stuck. A very basic affirmation like, "just think positively and you can do anything," could easily become a weapon of intimidation.

To get control, we have seen how intimidator optimists use positive affirmations, quotes, and even popular usage to force someone else into a negative act. Moreover, unless you're placed on an equal footing to question and seek understanding (through the practice of reaching open consent), you'll find yourself constantly unprepared for what the intimidator throws at you. If it is not a positive one-liner employed under pressure, it will be something else.

Numbers

There's another practice used by intimidators: numbers. If they lack the guts to force, weed out and intimidate the offending "no" personality with straight linear conclusions that refuse outside relational context (witnessed in the use of forced affirmations); and if they don't have pumped-up positive pressure to intimidate with what sounds like every-day motivation, then they use numbers and the bottom line. These people can be kind with of political nature. They can even express regret and sorrow for the decision to let good people go, but they are still failures as leaders. They are number crunchers and spend more time looking at spreadsheets and financial projections than allowing more freedom to surface new ideas and offer creative innovations.

When the cash-flow is down and the economy is in the crapper, why let good people go, people who have proven themselves repeatedly? Here's an example from a nonprofit housing organization that was left in a bad fix. When I was hired as an on-site construction supervisor, I found a mess. Invoices from new construction projects were tossed in a cabinet with no organization. State and federal agencies placed the program on high risk and they shut down the grant and placed the non-profit on probation. The CEO then fired the construction manager for failing to follow through with many code requirements and moved me into his position. With no director over me, I took the opportunity to organize everything for the first time. Outstanding invoices were paid, budgets matched real-life demands, procedures were written down and followed, and every job site had an organized binder in the back office. In other words, systems were created. I was then promoted to the director position, all within three months of being hired.

After the second year, just when everything was working in the black, a new business idea came to mind that would help make the organization more sustainable with less dependency on federal grants. I presented it to the CEO, and within three months I was terminated: economic advisors said the idea would have saved the organization.

A month after my release, the business idea became a finalist in a speed-pitch competition. As of today, the non-profit is out of business due to an uninformed board letting the CEO manage without the involved consent of his staff. As for the business venture, it inspired several ventures thereafter. After I was let go, the staff was all on board to give a certain project back to the bank. The CEO chose not to do this and the debt load eventually collapsed the non-profit. The nonprofit never built a team in full consensus. Instead, it was managed alone from the desk of one CEO with a board of directors that never really understood its role as a business first. Again, the CEO is a kind man, he even sacrificed much of his financial well being for the organization, but alone without giving consent to the informed staff, the ship runs amuck under the weight of authority knows best because the leader chose to do what the numbers said and not what ideas were telling him.

It takes massive strength in vision, tactical management, and knowledge of details to guide a company: that's too much for one person to handle alone with success. Many will disagree, but it is true. Nonetheless, we continue to build organizations on this model, with great power held in one person.

We can understand a cash-flow problem existing in any organization, and we can understand the decision to let certain people go. But why hire an outside consulting team to help structure an organization to be more sustainable? This is what happened after I was let go. We hire consultants and replace higher-paid staff with lower-paid staff because we hope to find a new administrative model or some new *best* practice to employ.

All we want is a better way to skim the milk. It's a numbers game. The problem is rarely cash flow but rather a lack of applied common consent in the organization. The problem is the shutting down of discussion that could surface new and better ideas. The problem is not letting everyone carry the weight of uncertainty and possible collapse.

Organizations fail to mature into more value because of a lack of discussion bringing the whole into one visionary drive. Discussion may require a lot of time to work out, but as a team, genuine people face the inevitable and solve problems together. Had the nonprofit's employees worked together in common consent, where dissent received encouragement, poor decisions could have been avoided, and the organization could have remained in operation—anyway who knows what might have happened?

As a team, either people come together or they break apart. Amazingly, we never choose a model that brings a team together. While seeing a team break apart is often the result of executive decision-making or the power center of one intimidating personality, coming together requires an organizational model that allows the whole team to fight through the disagreements and become better for it. Susan Scott in *Fierce Conversations* talks about this challenge at length. Every business leader should read it. At the very least, more leaders could present problems openly to the staff and let them carry some of the load in finding better solutions. The surprising effect is more unity and a connection that makes for a thriving culture.

Leadership Mess

Any good leadership publication teaches that all successful organizations guide themselves through a compelling vision. This is only a minor part. The real truth has to do with the source of vision. The best vision comes from the open range and never from a constricted feedlot. Jim Collins, in his book *Good to Great,* reveals how vision is best surfaced. "..we would debate, disagree, pound on tables, raise our voices, pause, reflect, debate some more, pause and think, discuss, resolve, question, and debate yet again...."[2] Because leaders don't require a genuine vision from a wider field of open consent, there's a collapse in leadership at every level of society. It is not the vision the leader gives that makes a great organization, it's the vision that everyone can get on board and make happen.

Without a well-defined vision from as many relational data points as possible, fake optimists fear vocal dissent and they do everything in their power to control this dissent. All this happens because they have no vision from which to "come out from behind themselves and into the conversation."[3]

Leadership today is failing to manage real diverse conversations to garner strategic direction. This is why best practices are eluding us. It's why there is no advanced technology to replace our leadership problems, and why we avoid experienced and hardworking staff that can offer key points to give greater consensus to the organization. Opening the conversation to greater consent does not mean we need to cow-tow to identity or sensitivity training. It just means, there is a problem in logistics, product quality, or in the basic communication flow. Essentially, there is a failure to put all the solutions on the table that solve real needs.

We have shut down this entire process because limiting access is the control model and not the living and thriving model found in greater open communication. This is all made worse with the fear of political correctness rearing its ugly head about some issue unrelated to the culture we are trying to build. We fear individual rants against the organization for assumed biases and fail to focus on systems and processes that make an organization thrive. Both a rant and a new idea have the same emotional strength and we falsely associate the two as being the same.

Central to the intimidator optimist is a person or bureaucratic body using forced commands. Sometimes the force is direct and sometimes it's implied. Sometimes it's from the boss above and sometimes it's from the push all around.

As is true for the staged optimist, the only way to see this coercion is to have confidence in your own dissenting voice and a greater depth of meaning to support responsible action.

This brings up a point about the depth of meaning discussed thus far. If you don't have the optimism for dissent, which comes with having your own mind, you subject yourself to the intimidator. We call this the *Enjambment.*

The Enjambment

Back in the eighties, there was a baseball pitcher for the Los Angeles Dodgers named Fernando Valenzuela. He had a unique style of pitching that landed within the strike box but very close to the hitter's hands. If you can imagine hitting a baseball within inches of your hands and feeling the vibration of the ball hit way off-center, you can imagine a sudden shift in power the pitcher refuses to give away.

In poetry, that is called enjambment: the continuation of a sentence or clause over a line break. If a poet allows all the sentences in a poem to end in the same predictable place as regular line-breaks, or in the case of baseball a dead center strike, a kind of deadening can happen in the ear and the brain. If the language has the same length, then the thoughts will, too.

Enjambment is one way of creating audible interest, kind of like a sudden vibration from hitting a ball too close to your grip. Notice the intentional delay of emotion with a surprise effect in these two lines from Alexander Pope's *The Rape of the Lock*:

> On her white breast a sparkling cross she wore
> Which Jews might kiss, and infidels adore.

The second line confuses the reader with a question. Why would a Jew or infidel adore a cross? On second reading, the reader realizes that "breast" doesn't carry the general connotation of "chest" but instead the specific idea of a woman's breasts, which are so attractive that a man of any religion would kiss the Christian cross to be near them. The idea is to delay the intention of the first line until the following line plays on the expectation.

With intimidator optimists, they hide the intent. They put things to the far edge of outright intimidation while staying just far enough inside the authoritative strike range. The intimidating optimist delays the intent by covering the motive to control with the expectation of something positive. In sports this is competition. In relationships at work, home, school, and in the community, it's intimidation.

Every batter who stood against Valenzuela had to swing or strikeout. This defines the precise condition of everyone who's been politically intimidated by a fake optimist. The game of baseball is one thing, but the game of life doesn't work through enjambment. To delay truth until the expectation in poetry helps communicate the intent, but to hide motive follows the law of survival of the fittest—and not the higher law of freedom of dissent. The massive self-improvement and coaching industries do little to open lanes of dissent. They are mostly about hiding motive and focusing on the immediate transaction. Let's fire them all. They are too busy coaching others to stampede over slow-poke minds prone to thoughtful and patient innovation.

Genuine Dissent

Few people, if any, don't know what genuine dissent is, and this explains why the intimidator rises in leadership and the person of genuine encouragement does not. Political intimidators rise in leadership because we bury genuine optimism under the positive self-help movement in the same way Christianity buried true faith in the magic of free salvation. Both should be fired.

To an enjambment that intimidates, faith says, "no!" It's that simple. Faith does this with applied action that appears negative in the face of imposed control. In truth, it is genuine, neither positive nor negative, just honest. Often, we don't see intimidating control until it's too late. This is why we have to swing or strikeout. No matter how we look at it, we box ourselves in, and we don't know how to get out without knowing our own minds. One of the only ways to know our own mind is to employ an enjambment *no*! It is how Fernando Valenzuela was so successful, he said no to how everyone else was pitching. Raised in poverty in Mexico and without the influence of someone telling him how the professionals do it, he was able to invent his own way—the enjambment no in a unique pitching style.

Take the meaning of democracy. Is it just a vote you make in a private booth with no responsibility to engage in social discourse? This is what it has become, but this isn't the origin of democracy. The word comes from the Greek (*dēmokratía*) that means "rule of the people," which was in turn derived from (*dêmos*) "people" and (*kratos*) "power" or "rule."

These are still unclear until we get to *self-rule*, *self-determination* and *equal say*, all of which stand in greater opposition to (*aristocratic*) "rule of an elite."

If we say that democracy is a popular government by majority rule, it doesn't properly stand in opposition to aristocratic elitism. In other words, the more we define democracy within the context of individual consent, the closer we get to the natural optimism of an enjambment no with no intimidation.

The idea of democracy is not merely a vote but a discussion that people engage in prior to and after voting. Over time, intimidating powers have led us into *linear* boxed-in voting without any local discussion. At the same time, we have lost the social discourse found in *relational* connections that lead to greater consent and a highly informed citizenry. In other words, we all want to challenge each other's vote with our voice. Take away each other's voice and give everyone just a vote and we empower elitists, biased media, money powers and leadership icons with greater command in their own voice to manipulate the vote. Both vote and voice must be kept together, in the same room, face-to-face, and ruled by the highest level of consent we dare demand. Welcome to the foundation of a new renaissance that will fire everything that is fake in how we organize today.

Political intimidators make themselves the gatekeepers of all social discourse. They seek to control all voices. Our everyday business meetings follow the same methodology—they too often avoid, dampen, and control discussion to give more to central power figures commanding majority rule. The result is that natural relational connections are put aside in favor of linear and purely mechanical conclusions.

The challenge we face is how to reopen the gates of social discourse to reach greater consent. This is optimistic. Creating this kind of freedom is an enjambment to intimidating optimists rather than *their* enjambment to our lack of faith.

The Open Forum

As intimidators work to control our minds while sitting in a cubicle, they'll never control the community forum at its lowest level—the level of gossip. If we could rise to a higher level than gossip with the power of horizontal consent in modular form, we could change the world.

Pushing for more open forum expression with real teeth in consent is the only social enjambment there is against the centralization of political control. We can do this by removing our need for central power and replacing it with a much wider, horizontal voice of consent.

A wise hitter can reposition his stance and open the swing of his bat to increase his chance of a solid hit. Open discussion in which everyone has a chance to speak is the honest way of repositioning our stance. If everyone had an equal voice in modular assemblies of common consent, the true meaning would arise, and everyone would begin to see the fake optimist standing naked. You don't even need to talk about intimidation—you just need to push for the consent of everyone involved to reveal the intimidator who demands full and central control.

If everyone responds to a meaning that's slightly different from that of the intimidator, the intimidator will select a new saying to keep false control through majority rule. The process will go round and round until the intimidator finally changes his pitch.

Supporting more consent through discussion is the true enjambment for fake optimists hiding in a central control booth. Intimidators avoid freedom because open and honest discussion requires more responsibility from everyone, which means no idolatrous worship of controlling authority. Using the same character keywords as we used with staged optimists, notice the traits associated when it comes to intimidators. When it comes to idolatry, where staged optimists sought for glory, intimidating optimists seek for control. The motive of the intimidator is control and their reward is obedience. **See Figure 2-1**.

Fig. 2-1 Traits of the Intimidating Optimist

Character	Traites
Idolatry	Seeks Control
Intelligence	Glory in Power
Agency	No Freedom
Motivation	Control
Reward	Demads Obedience

When we study intimidation as a fake optimism that is always held in the power center and never in the people, the staff, or the team, we can see the reason for a better model. A better model, even a superior democratic process, will include the application of responsible faith that allows everyone involved the genuine optimism of common descent. If we don't have expressed disagreement in common, we can't have a consensual agreement in common. This logic has been rejected for way too long as a vital part of any democracy, mainly because it is the true spirit of a republic.

Put another way, when we take the magic out of faith, we inject responsibility. When we take the power struggle out of optimism, we inject common consent.

Intimidation is a compulsory *yes* and it will never replace the responsibility inherent in *no*. The force of yes, if unchecked over time, works against the negation of no. This is where the binding optimism of the intimidator's words refuse to hear dissent by lumping all expressions of disagreement into ignorance, insubordination and direct disobedience.

When Christ responded to the stoning of a prostitute, skilled protesters used the linear conclusions from the law to support their actions. As the most powerful human enjambment against their intimidation, Christ said, "Let he who is without sin cast the first stone." In one phrase, Christ gave everyone the freedom to continue stoning the woman based on the law, but now they understood their true responsibility—and their true motive. They fired themselves.

In dealing with intimidating optimists, it helps to learn two kinds of enjambment no. The first is the intelligent *no* that challenges authority just by asking questions. Second is the defiant *no* that dissents directly against authority and tradition. When a hesitant *no* surfaces, there's usually intelligent cause for it. If there's no way to express disagreements, defiance will creep in and eventually, this leads to revolution, revolt, and the reorganization of power. In time, the *intelligent no* will always lead to the *defiant no* if not allowed free expression.

Sometimes this can have dire consequences. Consider President Kennedy's intelligent no given in an address before the American Newspaper Association on April 27, 1961:

> You may remember that in 1851 the New York Herald Tribune under the sponsorship and publishing of Horace Greeley, employed as its London correspondent an obscure journalist by the name of Karl Marx.
>
> We are told that foreign correspondent Marx, stone broke, and with a family ill and undernourished, constantly appealed to Greeley and managing editor Charles Dana for an increase in his munificent salary of $5 per installment, a salary which he and Engels ungratefully labeled as the "lousiest petty bourgeois cheating."
>
> But when all his financial appeals were refused, Marx looked around for other means of livelihood and fame, eventually terminating his relationship with the Tribune and devoting his talents full time to the cause that would bequeath the world the seeds of Leninism, Stalinism, revolution and the cold war.
>
> If only this capitalistic New York newspaper had treated him more kindly; if only Marx had remained a foreign correspondent, history might have been different. And I hope all publishers will bear this lesson in mind the next time they receive a poverty-stricken appeal for a small increase in the expense account from an obscure newspaperman.[4]

As we become more confident about speaking out, intimidation will wane. We just need to encourage more questions, questions that require all to define meaning more clearly. This helps us say *no* with more confidence rather than force a *yes* with no hearing. If it's expressed in an open meeting, mildness will be like that of a batter taking a slightly different stance. Other people will begin to appreciate this as we obtain their unconscious consent.

Had Karl Marx been included in a model of open consent early in his formative years and throughout his career, who knows what he would have produced? He might have preserved the value of freedom and attacked capitalism from a uniquely free-enterprise position at a community level and not from his Platonic state-run need for central control.

Corporations and large institutions should understand that leadership's enemy is the intimidator because intimidators eliminate independent minds quickly. Consider any new manager hired with a hopeful attitude and a successful past. This new manager comes aboard, willing to think and speak openly and honestly, but the manager will eventually leave when intimidators (from above) combine with intimidating employees (below). When the upper management controls through intimidation, most likely the bulk of the employees find a status-quo niche of self-protection, a perfect excuse to keep from bearing any greater responsibility.

When we easily accept the traditional policy and don't allow anything new to enter the domain, intimidating leaders force us and we either become part of the sickly whole—or we leave. A constant change in managers and high turnover is a sign of intimidation and the eventual fall of any organization.

Governments, on the other hand, don't fall as readily because they naturally breed political opportunists who combine in secret adulation for each other to get more control. The citizen isn't the one who causes this lust for control. Citizens just allow it by giving up their voices to a popular democracy where majority rules and full consent of the governed is silenced. When we lose our consent to central powers, we empower them with the ability to sow discord for more control. Thomas Paine had something to say about this:

> Men in all countries who get their living by war, and by keeping up the quarrels of nations, is as shocking as it is true; but when those who are concerned in the govern- ment of a country, make it their study to sow discord, and cultivate prejudices between nations, it becomes the more unpardonable.[5]

Thomas Paine

Governments eventually become intimidating by sow- ing discord between nations—and discord inside their borders. With the reach of the Internet and the rise of the alternative media, this has become an increasing challenge for governments to stage a crisis and create division among the people for more control.

In fact, at no other time in history has the world been so politically awake as now. Staging false crises is almost impos- sible with so many independent media outlets ready to report clear facts and answer the hard questions. Like the increase of freedom that occurred with the printing press, the increase of freedom never had a second wind until the birth of the Internet.

Make no mistake; corporate and government powers continue to look for ways to put controls on this new freedom of dissent. Eventually they will be successful, and it is happening now in the following way: first, everyone is enticed onto large social media platforms where they are paid to produce content. Next, the demonetization of certain content producers with no explanation. This stops these creators from making a living from their content. Then their content is labeled hate speech and they are entirely banned and completely de-platformed across all so- cial media. We are at the final stages of this transition. Soon will come a revolt and a new foundation for more diverse freedom with social responsibility kept in local hands in order to con- serve voice in the same.

There will be no guns, no civil war, and no uprising against the controlled establishment. There will be instead a new founding of social consent from the bottom up, the long-awaited decentralized renaissance of humanity. In other words, people will learn to organize once again and in very unique and decentralized ways.

In the near future, there will be a power shift in social responsibility. Local organized bodies will rise, most likely in private models, and they will take incremental accountability for the health, education, and welfare of each other—and that's only the beginning, and it will happen in very troubling times. Such times could be a severe economic downturn or a combination of several factors. Next will come greater common vision and the abolition of central authority. In other words, the next foundation of humanity's progression toward liberty is going to be quite literally inaccessible to fake optimists. By placing more responsibility in the hands of local modular groups, a powerful form of wide dissent can take place. But first, we need to begin asking real questions.

Standing in Dissent

To understand the power of voicing dissent against intimidating powers, look at the unintended consequences of blowback.

Blowback is what governments and even corporations suffer from when their actions reveal their deception. A good example is when the Secretary of Defense for the United States, Donald Rumsfeld, said—with a straight face, in front of news reporters and with certainty—that "Iraq has weapons of mass destruction." Only in hindsight and with free access to the Internet do we see how he was polished in both his stance and his communication skills. There was no connection between what he said and the truth.

At the time, most people believed that the invasion of Iraq after 911 was right, yet at the same time, there were a substantial number of dissenting voices that were ignored. Very few asked why in public because the upsurge of *no* was shadow-boxed into a corner. The Secretary of Defense was not allowing questions of dissent to surface in the discussion. He deflected real concerns with more forced optimism imposed by his authority rather than allowing for open discourse.

He used phrases such as "this is complicated," "honorable people are in charge," and, at one time on February 12, 2002, when he addressed the lack of evidence linking the government of Iraq with supplying weapons of mass destruction to terrorist groups, he said:

"These are things we know that we know. There are known unknowns. That is to say, there are things that we know we don't know. But there are also unknown unknowns. There are things we don't know we don't know."[6]

A reporter then asked, "Is this an unknown?" Hidden in this same obscurity the reporter was asking, "Is this an unknown threat?"

Rumsfeld then said in reply, "I am not going to say which it is."

When we challenge a soft-pedaling intimidator optimist in open public, he rejects clarity and uses his position of power to shut down access to intelligent reasoning. It's almost impossible to stand against this person face-to-face alone, but in the open, the target is yours if you dare take it. And when you dare take it, you will be labeled and marginalized, and finally censored. Look at Candice Owens and Brandon Straka, both were devout liberals in the Democrat party and then left to found two movements, Blexit, and #WalkAway. They stood alone for what they believed and then they were attacked. Because their voices of dissent do not fit within the narrative that a black woman or a gay man can become conservatives, they are vilified by intimidating progressives who need to continue labeling all conservatives as racist, bigoted, homophobic, fascists and Nazis.

Unfortunately, fewer and fewer people are willing to take the shot against intimidation. This is what happens with so many reporters today. A great number of them shut down their responsibility to ask questions of meaning and only one—if we're lucky—stands in opposition. When such a person stands alone, we must take notice. We must see that this person isn't wearing the fashion of idolatry for the collective hierarchy of appeasement. He learns and listens carefully and is willing to risk everything, but only if he is truly standing alone. This is the real difference. You cannot claim to have an independent voice if you are under a source of intimidation which you are seeking favors from.

Take WikiLeaks's founder Julian Assange. While many have labeled him a traitor and shouted that he should be punished for simply posting classified information that was leaked to him by a genuine whistleblower, nobody has proven his motive to get gain of any kind. Assange has stood alone and willingly subjected himself to isolation for many years. Truly independent enjambment personalities exist. They have no agenda other than revealing the truth. To assume there is a personal gain in revealing the corruption of others is to assume a very narrow understanding of one's humanity inside the lonely sacrifice of those willing to stand alone. Is he a staged optimist seeking attention? No! How do we know? Because he invites full access to his mind and inspires open inquiry, meaning he willingly takes questions from others. Is he an intimidating optimist? No! He does not shut down discourse of any kind. Is he another form of fake optimism? Maybe, but this much we do know, once you see how fake optimists evade open access to genuine questions, you will see Julian Assange is not fake at all.

For an example of shutting down open discourse by an intimidating optimist, consider a heated dialogue that took place on July 1, 2009, between White House press secretary Robert Gibbs and veteran White House correspondent Helen Thomas. The debate surfaced when Chip Reid, a reporter, was challenging the lack of transparency and openness the administration had campaigned for. Gibbs had an exchange involving Reid and Thomas that went as follows:[7]

Gibbs: "… But, again, let's—how about we do this? I promise we will interrupt the AP's tradition of asking the first question. I will let you (Chip Reid) ask me a question tomorrow as to whether you thought the questions at the town hall meeting that the president conducted in Annandale—"

Chip Reid: "I'm perfectly happy to—"

Helen Thomas: "That's not his point. The point is the control"

Reid: "Exactly."

Thomas: "We have never had that in the White House. And we have had some, but not—this White House."

Gibbs: "Yes, I was going to say, I'll let you amend her question."

Thomas: "I'm amazed. I'm amazed at you people who call for openness and transparency and—"

Gibbs: "Helen, you haven't even heard the questions."

Reid: "It doesn't matter. It's the process."

Thomas: "You have left open—"

Reid: "Even if there's a tough question, it's a question coming from somebody who was invited or was screened, or the question was screened."

Thomas: "It's shocking. It's really shocking."

Gibbs: "Chip, let's have this discussion at the conclusion of the town hall meeting. How about that?"

Reid: "Okay."

Gibbs: "I think—"

Thomas: "No, no, no, we're having it now--"

Gibbs: "Well, I'd be happy to have it now."

Thomas: "It's a pattern."

Gibbs: "Which question did you object to at the town hall meeting, Helen?"

Thomas: "It's a pattern. It isn't the question—"

Gibbs: "What's a pattern?"

Thomas: "It's a pattern of controlling the press."

Gibbs: "How so? Is there any evidence currently going on that I'm controlling the press—poorly, I might add."

Thomas: "Your formal engagements are pre-packaged."

Gibbs: "How so?"

Reid: "Well, and controlling the public—"

Thomas: "How so? By calling reporters the night before to tell them they're going to be called on. That is shocking."

Gibbs: "We had this discussion ad nauseam and—"

Thomas: "Of course you would because you don't have any answers."

Gibbs: "Well, because I didn't know you were going to ask a question, Helen. Go ahead."

Thomas: "Well, you should have."

Reporter: "Thank you for your support."

Gibbs: "That's good. Have you e-mailed your question today?"

Thomas: "I don't have to e-mail it. I can tell you right now what I want to ask."

Gibbs: "I don't doubt that at all, Helen. I don't doubt that at all."

Helen Thomas, age 89 at the time, had covered the White House during every presidency since John F. Kennedy. Later, in an interview with CNN, Helen said, "Not even Richard Nixon tried to control the press the way President Obama is trying to control the press. Nixon didn't try to do that," Thomas said.

"They couldn't control (the media). They didn't try." Thomas also said, "They're supposed to stay out of our business. They are our public servants. We pay them." Helen retired shortly thereafter with a note of dissatisfaction that her life's work had ended bitterly. Thomas stood alone, with no group-think intimidation pushing her.

When you compare Helen Thomas to Jim Acosta, both White House reporters for their respective news outlets, the tables are suddenly turned. Jim Acosta becomes the intimidator reworking language to a political end by questioning whether or not there is a true emergency at the border. President Trump then scolded CNN's Jim Acosta during the President's Rose Garden announcement on February 15, 2019, in which he called for a national emergency on the southern border and then told Acosta that he has "an agenda," and that "you're CNN, you're fake news."

For years illegal immigration has been an issue with both political parties calling for better immigration practices and better support at the southern border, but with a completely irreverent and independent enjambment in the presidency called Donald Trump, his efforts to secure the border were labeled an "immorality." And because he wants better support at the border, he is called xenophobic and racist. So what is the real agenda? Who benefits with an open border policy? The Democratic party benefits because traditionally the vast majority of illegal aliens, immigrants, and various minorities vote for Democrats. Therefore, if your agenda is to flood the country with immigrants from south of the border in order to get more votes, or if your agenda is to destabilize the United States for some hidden intent, you can't say this is your goal openly, so you attack those trying to secure the border by calling them everything in the book. You then assume a higher moral ground, but in truth, you appeal to the collective establishment of power. You become an intimidating optimist; your motive is hidden while your words are fake in their assumed optimism for some abstract global good.

No matter the discomfort, truly enjambment personalities willing to stand against intimidating labels eventually excel in an open forum where consent is naturally promoted through free inquiry. We can't shut dissent out with the positive force of controlled intimidation just to avoid confrontation. If we do let this happen, we leave a door open for the abuse of power to enter. For example, Freshman congresswomen Alexandria Ocasio-Cortez (AOC) can easily say in a live Instagram video that "The United States is running concentration camps on our southern border." Then later she can say they are being forced to "drink out of toilets." Is any of this true? Please check for yourself. Do not accept what one media outlet says, check multiple and alternative media sources to get not just a wide cross-section, but a deeper understanding of motive fueled by hatred and perhaps divisiveness created to get more power.

Intimidators get power when nobody calls them out. The problem is intimidators can easily get others to back them up through mutual adulation. This is what AOC did, in June 2019 she retweeted several prominent personalities all supporting her claims, but what was their motive? Do their words make AOC's claims any truer? No! But that does not matter because the majority works by linear means, they assume what others say is true rather than what they find on their own through relational inquiry and completely free of any bias.

What is true is that we are facing cultural and corporate censorship of individual voice at a level, Hitler, Mao, and Stalin could only dream of having. A gay conservative man, Milo Yiannopoulos, is rejected from speaking at UC Berkeley in 2017, and a gay Asian reporter who leans conservative, Any Ngo, is brutally attacked in Oregon for reporting on ANTIFA behavior in 2019. These are two stories from countless actions of intimidation against many in America today. Independent citizen journalists that lean right are being demonetized and de-platformed from across all social media because they do not support a certain intimidating agenda. The faceless collective hierarchy of forced pollical correction, which is always a moving target inspired by mutual adulation, is a fake optimism of *yes* rejecting the natural dissent of *no*.

In looking back, the entire war in Iraq, the war in Afghanistan, the war on drugs, the war on poverty, and even the Vietnam and Korean wars, were all forced on Americans with no room for opposition or debate. For example, no matter how justified the war in Iraq sounded after the attack on Sept 11, 2001, something was not right. It was not until this war that many Americans began to wake up to the historical record that certain powers either foment war to get gain or they create the environment for future revolutions that cause a war between countries, or strife in a corporation. It is time we all wake up so we can fire those who seek to repeat history over and over again.

Humanity does not inherently repeat itself over and over, certain powers utilize manipulative means to repeat history. It is how we organize that causes history to repeat, and not how we are as a people. *The High Road* that will come will explain it all.

Sowers of Discord

Here is a fact. We can trace the beginning of World War II to the Versailles Treaty, an unjust imposition placed on the German people for causing and losing World War I. It forced a huge burden of war reparations (debt to be paid in cash, cattle, and natural resources), which obliterated German sovereignty and essentially kept Germany from becoming an industrial power. Hitler came on the scene only after the Treaty of Versailles. World War II grew out of a despot willing to say no to a repressive treaty imposed by outside powers that gave no voice and no recourse to the German people, essentially no ability to say no intelligently.

We point a finger at Hitler, who truly deserved to die, yet we refuse to blame Woodrow Wilson of the U.S, David Lloyd George of Britain, and Georges Clemenceau of France, who together imposed the treaty. Together they sustained the impoverishment and economic collapse of Germany after the first war in the same way hoodlum gangs pillage store shops during a community crisis. This angered the German people enough to follow a crazy man to stop the global confiscation of their resources.

When we refuse open free expression and force corrupt controls on people without their consent, eventually they will say no, first intelligently and then violently. Sometimes that revolt swings too far and they create another despotic intimidating government that refuses to hear dissent against itself. Such was the case with Hitler, and it continues with the adulation engineering we see in all bureaucracies. Put a dreadful tyrant full of lies and false promises in office and enough of the majority will cow-tow to him to advance their position. We now call this the deep state. An older term is called social protectionism. Genuine optimists willing to say no in direct dissent are suddenly out-numbered, ridiculed, and marginalized. Again, this is so much easier to see than trying to follow the money or reveal a smoking gun behind mass corruption. For a massive example, read *Wild Swans: Three Daughters of China* by Jung Chang, a documented example of adulation engineering by a majority controlled by one single intimidating optimist who led the way to nearly seventy million of his citizens murdered by the hand of his worshipers.

A forced direction without wide and distributed consent and with no opportunity for redress of grievances produces war, injustice, poverty, and inequality. What are the powers pushing for in an entire nation? It's the powers wanting resources—and, perhaps, the imposition of austerity measures to tax the people directly under a false optimism of carbon taxation said to save the planet. Offshore banks hold veto power over governments, not with guns, but with foreign debt. This merely forces social and internal expenditure-cutting to pay the debt. In other words, austerity is often associated with a loss of sovereignty imposed by outside thugs. We see this problem in countries that are required to give away their independence due to the debt they owe to foreign banks.

If people want war, it's because of the propaganda of injustice. The real motive comes from economic powers that stand to benefit. Only they can manipulate leaders to give fake promises that incur more debt. Only those who truly benefit have the motive for pushing the public narrative by instigating false political events called false flags. These are staged events blamed on a political enemy to start a war or enact draconian laws in the name of security or some assumed moral cleansing.

For instance, in 47 BC, Julius Caesar used a series of riots and arson attacks—that he paid for and commanded—to destabilize the Roman Republic before marching his legions across the Rubicon and into Rome, where he took power and declared himself emperor.

In 64 AD, Emperor Nero deliberately allowed Rome to burn in a series of arson attacks to blame them upon the emerging Christian sect. This set Christians up for persecution as enemies of the state, thus enabling their bloody genocide and a very convenient deflection away from the intent of established powers to limit access to resources and assets. The greater the scarcity of resources the more wealth is created for the haves against those who have not.

Hitler capitalized on seizing more power when, in 1933, it is said Rohm's SA set fire to the Reichstag (German Parliament) which allowed Hitler to blame it on the Communists, thus enabling him to crack down on his main political rivals and construct his police state in post-Weimar Republic Germany. It does not matter if Marinus van der Lubbe, a Dutch communist, said he alone set fire to the German Reichstag building on 27 February in 1933. The event was used to instigate political control, bloodshed, and war.[8] A crisis is always great theater for grabbing more political control, and always for some assumed good to hide a hidden intent.

Over time, we'll eventually begin to see more false-flag events, either planned or not, which are used to centralize more power and more control, all under the guise of being the good thing to do while under the spell of intimidation. Even the

Patriot Act of 2001 had over 360 pages supposedly written in just days after the 911 events. This begs suspicion that it was pre-written and waiting for the right crisis to come along. And when the right crisis came, those ready to make billions in the new police state at airports and in mass surveillance technology stood ready to profit. All false flags stem from secret combinations of power ready to profit. The new crisis suddenly allows intimidation of dissent to rise in ways we never thought possible. If you don't see history repeating itself, then look at the staged performances of some leaders who remove themselves from open questions or look for the one in control trying to shut down discussion. This is so much easier to spot than trying to follow the money or prove a conspiracy.

God may punish His children for the sins of their fathers, but this is just a promise to us as parents that the despots we choose will bring darkness, poverty, and ignorance to our children until we wake up again. What is it that we cannot see? What enjambment no do we not allow to rise naturally every time intimidating powers set out to control us?

Fighting for Disagreement

I spent some time talking to an army officer who had recently returned from Afghanistan. He had top-secret clearance in both Afghanistan and Iraq. I asked him a simple question: "What is the problem with Afghanistan?"

He replied with certainty, "Natural gas and opium."

He mentioned the energy companies involved and, without any political opinion, he continued to suggest that we sustain war when there are natural resources to obtain, especially energy, currency manipulation, and black-market resources. While this is not a tremendous revelation to many who know better, it is certainly news to the majority controlled by intimidating optimists.

Look at the government bailouts in the United States in 2008 and 2009, and the quantitative easing that continued for years after. When private banks and corporate combines of power get to print money to pay for their losses, we are told the sky will fall and major depression will happen if we do not prop up those that are too big to fail. So instead we just make these cartels of collusion bigger by giving them direct access to printing money to pay their debts. With trillions of dollars, we magically push away the fear of a total economic collapse.

We witness over and over the same rush to solve, in fear, some pending doom manufactured out of thin air. If you want to understand intimidation, just look at how fast things happen in Congress during a crisis and then look at where the money goes. It does not matter if the crisis is a conspiracy by powers in government or not. A crisis is used by fake optimists to profit and grab more control.

After the bailouts that began in 2009, trillions found their way into offshore banks. It's no different from a mob shakedown of local businesses in the name of protection racketeering, the most insidious form of intimidation under the guise of security. The only difference now is that we're experiencing global racketeering.

If you don't believe me, read *Confessions of an Economic Hit Man* by John Perkins, or *The Crime of Our Time* by Danny Schechter. Nomi Prins also has a lot to say in her book *It Takes a Pillage* and in her later book, *All the Presidents' Bankers*. Consider also Ellen Brown's massive research in her book *Web of Debt* or G. Edward Griffin's wildly successful *The Creature from Jekyll Island*. May I also suggest Catherine Austin Fitts' *Solari.com* and Max Keiser's *MaxKeiser.com*. I site these resources because the idea of global racketeering is not widespread in the mainstream media but thoroughly documented without the general public's knowledge.

We cannot assume that the dying mainstream media will report on this racketeering because they're stuck in a vertical power grid where dissenting minds remain suppressed while idolatrous minds reach higher plateaus while advancing more central control.

We see the mainstream media hiring the best staged and most intimidating optimists available, the kind of detached and inaccessible human beings who avoid taking questions from independent minds. It's no wonder that the alternative media is the new media. It's protecting the optimism of no and single-handedly preserving our freedom, but not for long.

The Optimism of No

The Peter Principle, published in 1969, explained why we have incompetent leadership. It argued that we are hierarchal by nature, whether patriarchal, feudalistic, capitalistic, or socialistic. Because of these hierarchies, every position of leadership falls to a person of incompetence so long as the powers above want them there.

Better reason can explain why this happens. Although we organize into hierarchies by default because of the nature of human idolatry, the incompetence of fake optimism grows out of the presumed safety of *yes* in one extreme rather than the uncertain dialogue of *no* at the other. People rise to incompetence because it is financially, politically, and psychologically safe for them to be there, and hierarchies support this design. However, it is much deeper than this.

Finding fault with leaders by blaming incompetent positions on vertical structures of power isn't the solution. We must see the psychology of fear that naturally buries disapproval of *no* under a forced agreement for *yes.*

Thomas Carlyle's novel *Sartor Resartus,* published in the mid-1800s, spoke of the everlasting *nay* coming before the everlasting *yea.* He was right, to a point. To express "No!" forces a more clarified "Yes!" Moreover, to see a greater affirmation in the positive requires a greater degree of responsibility in hearing the negative.

In other words, true optimism defines a negative *no* that gradually works toward a more responsible *yes. The Peter Principle* happens because we are irresponsible in our talk; we don't engage the negative out of fear of losing ground or suffering rejection for what we have accepted as a positive stand.

Fake optimists—and all intimidating leaders—see *yes* as easy and *no* as threatening. In a way, the stand for *no* resides on both sides of *yes*. Without the freedom to dissent before and after a confirmed yes, our system falls into the political agreement without the culture of consent.

If every media outlet allowed for all questions of dissent to rise, the people would eventually see the political standing against what is genuinely optimistic. The reason we don't include every dissenting voice is that hierarchies are byproducts of idolatry. Then comes Trump, a voice willing to say anything against the yes enforcers. Trump has become not just an expression of American self-interest, but he is, no matter how much you hate him or love him, a voice of individual dissent long lost in American politics.

The maze of politics, until Trump, was not a conscious conspiracy, but a structure of idolatry. You could see this in media organizations that would shy away from asking tough policy or philosophical questions, or in their refusal to research, and all this not because that's what the market wants, but because that's what the power centers want. Idolatry to leaders overcomes the independent will to disagree. The mainstream media gathers more fake optimists while pushing out those willing to report on dissenting views alone. Many of us have seen the duplicated talking points in video format copied from countless media sites, all reporting on the same thing and using the same narrative. We now see an interlocking hierarchy of idolatry for power over the media that is more pervasive than ever.

The world presents an infinite maze of hierarchies, and some say that if you follow the money, you'll see the real power. There's a better way. Follow the idolatry for authority managed by a despotic form of intimidating optimism.

The obedient subjects of central power have no idea of the real power they have. They're convinced by their leaders because, over time, they've earned a living from them. Just as a prostitute doesn't snitch on her pimp, the pimp protects the racketeer.

Follow the hierarchy around the world and neither the head nor the tail knows the truth. The tail can be in the underworld and the head can be part of the highest leadership of a foundation for some good. When you follow the idolatry, however, you no longer need to know the head or the tail—because you see the insidious whole in collective worship.

What's done in secret subverts openness and the real optimism of *no*. This is the way of intimidating optimists. They always push for limited access, centralization of control, and more vertical hierarchies. Knowing this, we don't condemn conspiracy theorists as modern-day heretics. We just get others to see the dangerous idolatry instead of trying to connect the dots.

If you're in a black poverty-stricken neighborhood and you say, "There's a higher probability of more black crime," it doesn't make you a racist. Trying to make all things alike and equal is dangerous to a free society. The problem is with our central power structures that foment division in governments, churches, educational institutions, and in the corporate world. We have to tolerate it in some businesses because of ownership, but the people own the government, members own the church, and students have a right to open lateral discussion. The fact that we allow central control to form into vertically removed power centers of intimidating optimism is simply intolerable.

Once we understand that vertical hierarchies with central control are the problem, we need to understand that every hierarchy will intimidate differently.

Karl Marx tried to destroy hierarchies altogether by replacing them with, "from each according to his abilities and to each according to his needs."[9] Although this expresses an attempt at equality, it uses a false cover of equality to suppress the opposition of "no" rather than continuing the debate and coming to an honest consensus.

Great-sounding ideals offer no recourse for dissent. They are used to silence opposition without any concession. We see this with progressive statists. If they can force, legislate, and coerce what they think is good (and if they can do it without a wide field of consensus), they don't mention that they're building a vertical hierarchy that will eventually change into a despotic power. Genuine optimists may see it, but the idolatrous follower doesn't.

This shows how intimidating optimism exhibits especially destructive tendencies that lean heavily on the side of social entropy. Stalin, Mao, and Hitler, the genocide of Pol Pot and many more have destroyed the lives of more than 100 million people in the last century alone, and the number, many say, will exceed 250 million when you include murder by government. According to an extensive research project conducted by Rudolph J. Rummel, Ph.D., "the less liberal the democracy and the more totalitarian a regime, the more likely it will commit democide (death by governments)."[10] He offers these points from his research:

- Freedom ameliorates the problem of mass poverty.
- Free people have little internal violence, turmoil, and political instability.
- Freedom is a method of nonviolence—the most peaceful nations are those whose people are free.[11]

Given this, we then must ask, "How do we increase freedom?" This is going to be a great challenge with the trend moving toward more intimidation and more hierarchies driven by more centralized control.

Intimidation in Hierarchies

The most striking trait of intimidators is that they make one feel stupid by pushing positive expectation and obligatory anticipation, like Mao's "Great Leap Forward" or a corporate branding that moves rapidly through new market studies, statistical analysis, visionary re-branding, peripheral goal-setting, and corporate as well as federal protocol designed to steer clear of intuitively honest queries. Even a public display of patience is a kind of optimism that hides the intimidation yet to come.

When Barak Obama's Healthcare Act came to full implementation, we began to experience the intimidation imposed on small businesses while seeing the many executive waivers Obama gave to big corporations and labor unions. At the same time, we completely lost the optimism presented in the first place. Most of us don't want to believe until it is too late.

Empires fall because they give too much responsibility to their leaders with the promise that the people would be kept safe or their rights protected. This is how important the freedom of dissent is. Only with the constant freedom to speak up against establishment powers do we have checks against undue encroachments and intimidation.

Read *The End of America, Letter of Warning to a Young Patriot* by Naomi Wolf. It is a warning about the responsibility required to keep dissent-free. If not, the optimism of a revolutionary *no* will call on the blood of our children to take it back.

The new intellectuals for social justice seem to forget this. They want to keep leading the charge for progressive change with new centralized models but refuse to maintain the freedom of dissent. They are linear destroyers of relational progress.

Love of free expression is almost silent within the statist mind, and long forgotten in the cornered self-interest of individualism. This has happened because the old liberals from the sixties, who once dared to say *no*, have evolved into the new establishment promising a new optimism of *yes* in the hands of the state. They've become the intimidators. And for the other, the very idea of democracy as a means to reach an agreement has lost its power when the individual is intimidated to conform into the vertical power structure. We must encourage every form of dissent against the statist as well as the individual mind that works constantly for central control.

Intimidating optimists remain at the heart of political power because they quell the real optimism that rises in the voice of dissent in favor of a more clarified yes. They are counter-intuitive. If a decision rests on their shoulders, this is one thing; but when they get others to commit to actions, not of their own logic, they command through pressure cloaked as confidence in your idolatry towards them. This subtle force excuses intimidators from assuming liability for their own decisions and leans on second-tier adulterous bureaucrats to make a stand, which they never do because they create the same pressure under them.

To feel and speak honestly are expressions of human intelligence, and both the staged performer and the verbal intimidator want to control at least one of them. The staged optimist wants to control how you feel, and the intimidator optimist wants to control when and what you can speak. Both need to be fired.

Here is how we battle the need for control. First, your own intelligence must express meaning within the context of responsible action. Second, the optimism of *no* must remain at your disposal and rise in open consent. A new model of governing power in all organizations—as seen in horizontal consensus—is required to make all this work properly. At Vision Impact Leadership, we are the most forward-thinking in organizational consensus. The models for creating more thriving cultures with less power struggle have only just begun. Soon there will be a day when fake optimists will have no means to empower themselves.

We've learned that fake optimists have a unique way of avoiding or controlling discussion. How we master honesty and responsibility to stand against them will surprise most of us.

Before we can launch a new renaissance in human organization, let's look at the last fake optimist known for the greatest destruction of free agency, the *irrational optimist*.

We all tend to alter the meaning of words to justify our worldview. One might feel guilty or jealous for any reason, but rather than accept the guilt, we change the meaning of words to curb our regret. If we do not alter the meaning of words to deflect their imposition on us, we simply avoid talking about them or we shut down all access to any peer review.

Samuel Louis Dael

3
The Irrational Optimist

Our positive cover often becomes our shield and concealment, a bastardly defense against sound understanding.
The negative thinker, on the other hand, may just be trying
to look at things more realistically.

Samuel Louis Dael

The Stubborn Mind

A father once said to his son, "Positive thinkers are negative bastards." To prove his point, he gave his son a copy of *How
to Cure Yourself of Positive Thinking*. After reading this book, it
became apparent to the young man that there was such a thing
as an irrational optimist. I was this young man.

Irrational optimists take something negative and make it
a positive through magical delusion. In the process, they reject
the same thing the intimidator rejects: the free expression of a
dissenting *no*.

The only difference between the intimidator and the irrational is that irrational optimists use the appeal of magic to get
their way instead of intimidation, or instead of a staged performance.

Most of us don't succumb entirely to irrational optimists
in the same way that a lot of people submit to intimidators or
a brilliant show. Instead, many of us succumb to an irrational
mind because we want to believe in their enchantment, and it's
easy to become a willing collaborator. And if we don't collabo-
rate, we have to stand against them.

We can all recognize (perhaps in hindsight) experiences we've had with an irrational optimist. My first experience came from meeting a friend's mom when I was in grade school. She had nine kids and the family lived in a human pigpen while running a poorly managed dairy farm. During the summer, dead flies crash-landed and buzzed everywhere, with carcasses constantly piling up on the window ledge and in the bottoms of light fixtures. In the winter, the kids tracked mud and manure everywhere in the home. They never vacuumed, and yet their mother presented a constant smile as if all is good even if everything is bad.

Some parents do a great job home-schooling, but this friend's mother believed she was protecting her kids from the evils of the world by keeping them home. She required very little schoolwork, and they had almost no gumption for anything. Consequently, they performed academically below their age level, protected by what their mother called the "armor of God." A few years later, my friend's father died because his mother believed that conventional medicine was inherently evil. At the time, I wondered what could possibly be wicked about a life-saving procedure to remove a cancerous growth on his back?

My father, a friend of the family, helped move her husband from one bed to another. Before he died, he was in a coma, his body riddled with cancer. None of this seemed to deter the wife, because she believed that "things happen for a reason," which translates into "bad things happen for our good." It wasn't until years later that my father was able to challenge her basic assumptions in our own home. After a long-heated debate, she screamed in quivering despair, "I just want to be told what to believe." Such a mind is likely to be seduced by irrational optimism. In her case, an action-less belief in the magic of "things happen for a reason" left her with no agency and no real applied hope.

When we subject our agency to outside control in the form of some magic that will solve all things, life acts upon us because we refuse to act in life. Only when we act responsibly can we say we have faith. At its base core, faith implies some degree of responsible action. If not, it is fake and subject to an irrational belief. Whether we define the action as personal action or social action, faith is responsible action. Notice how this gets the mind to focus on what is responsible and away from fastidious practices and fanatical doctrines that justify no action. Does this push us away from God? Definitely not! It brings us closer together, and is this not godly? In other words, is not the glory of God intelligence that cleaves to intelligence?

When we hold to sound understanding, the irrational optimist cannot twist the meaning of faith into a magical solution without any responsible action. If we cannot focus on what is responsible, we cannot recognize what is irrational.

For example, Germany's last election until after the Second World War was held on 5 March 1933. Though the Nazis party won only 44% of the vote, Hitler persuaded the Reichstag (parliament) to pass a constitutional amendment called the Enabling Law, allowing him to govern independently for four years. Articles two and three of the enabling law read like this:

Article 2

Laws enacted by the government of the Reich may deviate from the constitution as long as they do not affect the institutions of the Reichstag and the Reichsrat. The rights of the President remain unaffected.

Article 3

Laws enacted by the government shall be issued by the Chancellor and announced in the Reich Gazette. They shall take effect on the day following the announcement unless they prescribe a different date.

Before the Enabling Act was passed, two vital things were needed. First, Hitler and his Nazi party needed to call the new law the "Law to Remedy the Distress of the People and the Reich." Keep in mind none of this would have happened without the confiscation and wealth imposed by outside nations. Positive-sounding titles are used to garner the approval of the people without their full knowledge of the new law. Second, he positioned soldiers outside the Kroll Opera House (temporary site of parliament) to make sure the legislature gave Hitler what he wanted. In one day Hitler employed both irrational denial and intimidating force, a very deadly combination. He should have been fired long before this. I reference Hitler's Germany because under great distress, people can easily subject themselves to tyrannical leaders because these leaders promise great salvation and even greater magic.

The key to recognizing irrational optimism is in the trait of denial of one's liberty that surfaces in how idolatry is expressed toward a new emperor. You can see this denial in how it quickly pushes aside dissent in favor of a new savior, state, empire, or new authority.

As the staged optimist expresses idolatry through glory, and as the intimidator expresses idolatry through control, the irrational optimist expresses idolatry through denial. Denial is the hardest trait to spot because it has the widest appeal to the greatest majority. Give the people an excuse to avoid taking responsibility, even allow them to vote themselves largess from the public treasury, and you gain control over their freedom. This is how destructive irrational optimism is. We see in trade unions, governments, and now corporations allowing to be subject to irrational magic to wash away personal and social accountability.

Other key traits of irrational optimist surface when aligned with the same character keywords to the left. Notice their character traits for reward and how they view intelligence. See **Figure 3-1.**

Irrational optimism seeks some traditional authority, political doctrine, or approval from God or the state to gain control; it ignores the still small voice within and the free agency of intelligence. The mother of my friend mentioned above never followed her heart, but rather followed certain authorities without knowing for herself. As positive as she was about her authoritative and often divine helplessness, there was no impetus from her own free will to do the optimum best thing. Many fanatic minds think that God rewards them for blind suffering.

Fig. 3-1 Traits of the Intimidating Optimist

Character	Traites
Idolatry	Denial
Intelligence	Glory in Self
Agency	Avoid Questions
Motivation	Social Exaltation
Reward	Social Worship

This is like saying God rewards people for enduring afflictions even without adding any value. Some religious people believe that "bad things" bring them closer to God. In no way can this idea be optimistic. Bad things happen to good people, and how we react to the bad to cope and get through the day determines our character and not how we accept a false idea of justice to wash away our sins.

Non-Responsive

In *Power vs. Force*, David Hawkins shares insights into the *frequencies* of human action. This image shows how human beings can vibrate at a much higher frequency than most people realize. **See Figure 3-2**.

The problem with irrational optimists is that they take something like Hawkins' research and keep it linear as if one frequency automatically leads to the next. Does pride lead to courage? Not all the time. Pride can easily regress and lead to anger if courage doesn't intervene. The same happens with love. What good is love, if we're not trying to reach greater enlightenment by tempering it with reason? This is not the real problem, though. The real problem is how on earth do we scale Hawkins' research? How do we genuinely adopt a path of more faith across society? As it stands, it seems non-responsive.

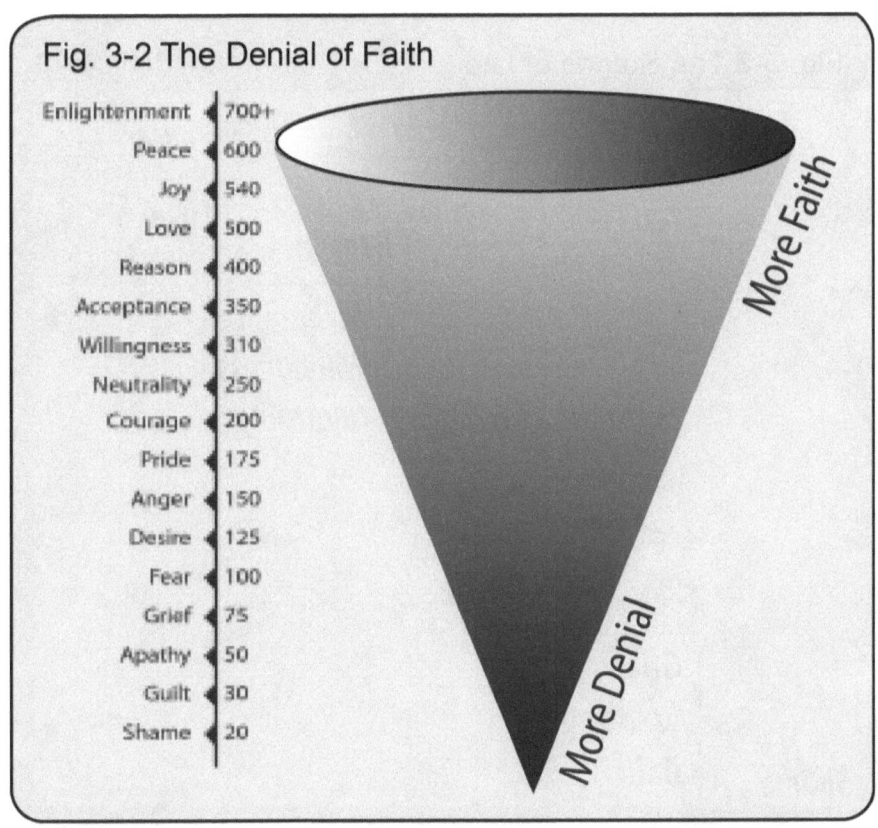

Fig. 3-2 The Denial of Faith

Enlightenment ◀ 700+
Peace ◀ 600
Joy ◀ 540
Love ◀ 500
Reason ◀ 400
Acceptance ◀ 350
Willingness ◀ 310
Neutrality ◀ 250
Courage ◀ 200
Pride ◀ 175
Anger ◀ 150
Desire ◀ 125
Fear ◀ 100
Grief ◀ 75
Apathy ◀ 50
Guilt ◀ 30
Shame ◀ 20

More Faith

More Denial

If you want answers, listen to an occasional podcast at genuineoptimist.com. There is a coming renaissance that will scale the real power of each person into the community. I call it *The High Road*.

When we step up in power, we have one foot on one step, and the other foot on a second step. This gives us stability. Irrational optimists never step up with stability. They stand still with both feet planted on one step. They look at pride, anger, and desire as a progressive movement toward rugged individualism. Or they look at guilt as if it is the same as acceptance. Most confusingly, the irrational optimist talks of enlightenment without the stability of reason or any need for courage. Optimism is all in their minds and never alive in every step they make in life. It's just one step and this is not genuine. **See Figure 3-3**.

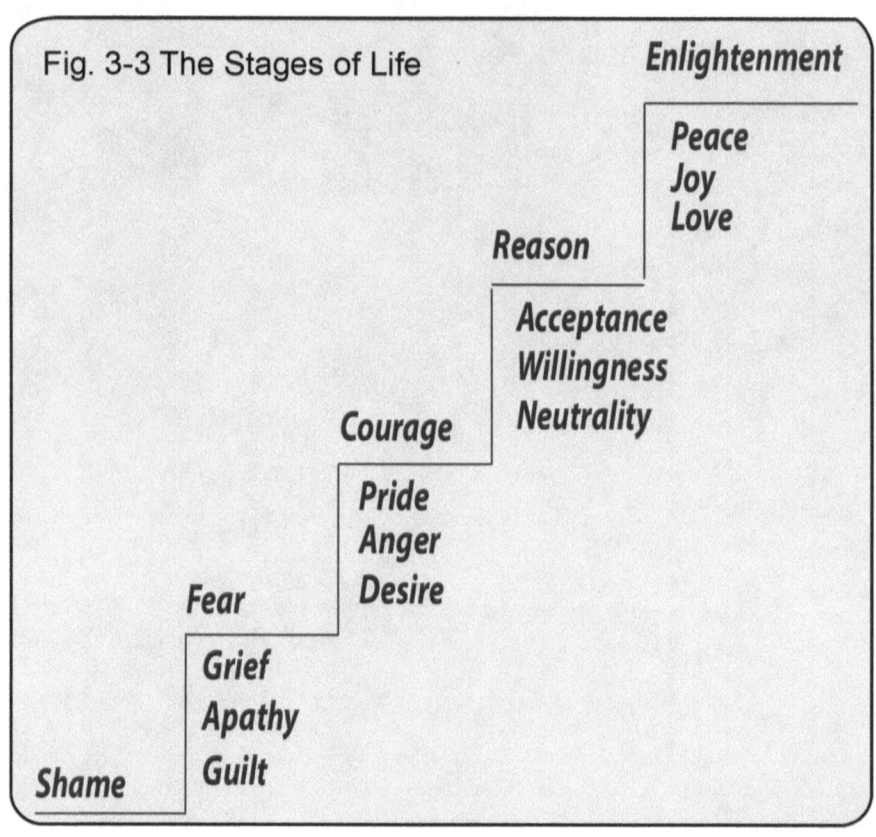

Fig. 3-3 The Stages of Life

Enlightenment

Peace
Joy
Love

Reason

Acceptance
Willingness
Neutrality

Courage

Pride
Anger
Desire

Fear

Grief
Apathy
Guilt

Shame

We used the word progressive above. Fake optimists will always claim they are progressive. How can this be when they are quick to shift responsibility onto the state or some other distant authority removed from a culture of consent? They never take responsible action themselves, which you would think best defines what it means to be progressive. They will centralize power and distance responsibility far away, and this is often repugnant to a genuine mind. Sometimes it's essential to be repugnant—the quality of being contradictory towards irrationality. This is necessary because the irrational optimist is skilled at diversions from responsibility. Contradictory repugnance becomes the only way to reveal the linear intolerance of the irrational mind.

For example, concerning the Jewish/Christian tithe, a confrontation erupted between an independent thinker and an economics professor. The economics professor was stuck in a linear intolerance imposed by the authority of his own religious culture. The Independent thinker was not. Watch how linear intolerance becomes non-responsive to a dissenting and intelligent no.

The two men were of the same religion, they were both Mormons. The professor, who was active in his church, came to the independent thinker to reactivate him. Over a period of months, the two men discussed their views on economics, and a discussion eventually led to a heated debate on the church's tithing method.

The thinker ran the numbers and showed how a father with four kids earning $28,000 a year pays $2,800 in tithing based on paying a tenth of his income. A single man with no kids pays $10,000 on $100,000 of his income. While the father of four rents and lives on $25,200, the other man lives on $90,000 and owns his home. If we adjust tithing to be 10% of one's net worth, as written in their own scripture (see Doctrine and Covenants 119), the father of four would pay much less, because he has very few possessions, and the rich man would suddenly pay on net worth annually. This follows the principle of paying a tenth of all possessions that Abraham paid to King Melchizedek, and not a tenth of one's income that many Christians follow today, especially Protestant Christians and Mormons.

According to the thinker, tithing by net worth decreases one's vanity for possessions and increases free enterprise, while tithing by income favors materialism and the gross nature of capitalism.

The economics professor then argued, "The church is led by men inspired by God." Do you see what happened? The professor killed the argument when he took his foot off reason and stepped back onto anger. This revealed his idolatry for religious authority. He became non-responsive to an *intelligent no*. In the forthcoming *The High Road*, the real truth of the Christian tithe if properly conserved within a closed community will be the foundation upon which a renaissance in liberty will form.

Reason always wins if one can set aside tradition and authority and replace both with good sense. Reason shared in an open body that can never be controlled by one person or discarded by a culture of force lifts us in the direction of love, joy, and peace. It adds enlightenment and inspires true collaboration. Irrationalism performs oppositely: it fosters central control and increases idolatry toward those in control. All it takes is the freedom to express an intelligent no.

When we choose not to act according to our defined values and prefer stubborn dogmatism, we manufacture an artificial direction to prove self-worth without considering the lack of good we add to the world. A daydream can be repugnant, but at times we use this to compensate for the irrationalism of day-to-day reality.

When we think our irrationalism is a valued principle, this is where the optimism of *no* must stand and call it out in free and open dissent. Perhaps we might even imagine how we could overcome the denial pushing an irrational thought process.

The Magic of Irresponsibility

Irrational optimists make choices that are often a denial of responsibility. Not surprisingly, they look optimistic while doing this. Let's look at it from a *deus ex machina* (god from the machine).

Anytime the plot of a Greek drama became too difficult to resolve, the playwright used a trap door or a crane behind the scenes to introduce a magical being who would jump into the confusing story and solve the crisis suddenly by magic.

We are all willing to suspend our disbelief in entertainment; there's nothing wrong with that. When it happens in life, however, we have a serious problem.

Consider the case of an irrational optimist who was the president of a company making millions of dollars by using anecdotal stories for their mineral packs that consumers would add to bottled water. As both a religious minister and the president of the company, he used the language of great promise (and no logic) to make his words stick. His mantra talked of the 97% who made less than $100,000 a year and how his network marketing company helped many of those 97% percent gain financial stability among the wealthy three percent. This is odd, since 97% of all those who join multi-level marketing companies fail. Nonetheless, the heavy coating of a staged optimism cloaked in revivalist rhetoric made it so that fewer than three percent of those present could see the dirty logic.

Infinite markets do not exist, and supply and demand will always control the movement of goods and services. Those facts were not part of this CEO's presentation. He believed that hundreds of thousands of independent sales agents all stepping over each other could fill the earth—and leave room for a billion more. The inherent lack of reason was eclipsed by the promise of personal gain. Costs are often more than thirty times the real value of the product in a multi-level marketing up-line. Not only do network-marketing companies sell value at very high prices; they push positive mental unrealities as if they were chewable vitamins.

This is how destructive motivational speakers can be when they begin to adopt irrational optimism. They use positive language in such a way that it gives the listener the escape from the responsible action they are seeking to avoid. It's such a poisonous form of hypocrisy that the modest heart cannot stand up and say, "No!" This problem is manifested in all of society that fears to stand up against irrational leadership built upon the worship of new magic or new authority. Our problem has always been that we lack genuine leadership that allows for open consent derived from the common agreement of all involved. We prefer the magic of the irrational to the responsibility of the Master.

Consider typical mental exertions of magic pushed by companies and compare them to what we simply understand as honesty. The difference is more than subtle.

The Fake

- Everyone needs this product
- Anyone can do this business
- We don't sell this business, we share it
- We have built your business for you

The Genuine

- Our product is not for everyone
- Nobody likes to sell but we can fill a need
- We are in the business of sales
- You build your own business

People who follow irrational optimists tend to have a mindset that gets fixated on forced magic to escape from taking active responsibility for being honest. Irrationalism feeds on an escape by appealing to other's fears and selling magic is the false confidence of choice. When you compare this to the knowledge and acceptance of one's own fear, you can see the denial in the irrational mind. In other words, the early Greek philosophers taught us to "know thyself." They taught this to keep the ravages of fear from taking hold of genuine purpose.

Remember, both faith and denial describe some kind of action. When we respond in fear, we are engaged in the denial of fear. When we react in faith, we are engaged in the acceptance of our fear. The second is a much higher value. Fear will always surface as denial or a raw disability, both are much lower values, unless dealt with intelligently by taking the steps from courage to reason and from reason to enlightenment. When we choose to act in faith, which we can simply call responsible action, fear dissolves and becomes less of a disability.

Something else is not quite clear. If fear is the motive for denial, what is the motive for faith? Faith is vital because irrational optimists exhibit an unreasonable faith. You can see this because irrational optimists avoid direct questions that confront their lack of responsibility. For instance, like any fake optimist, irrational minds lack depth; but, unlike intimidator optimists and unlike staged optimists, irrational optimists do not run from "no." Instead, irrational optimists co-opt the voice of no for their gain. It gives them the image of being open when in fact they are shut tight. It's like answering a question by saying, "Let me answer that by asking you this." In other words, they embrace *no* by turning it around and using it against you.

Momentum of Enthusiasm

Think of pushy salespeople trying to sell you something you neither need nor want. They appear to give lip service to your feelings (like the staged optimist), but they give absolutely nothing back (like the intimidator). People like this will give a great pitch, but when it comes time to allow others to act within their area of individual responsibility, irrational minds will shut it down every time.

For example, once we release a bowling ball, the best decision possible leaves our hand. If we see the ball going the wrong way, we don't waste energy running down the lane to correct the direction! And yet bad leaders do this constantly; they do not realize that every effort spent to correct the direction along the way will diminish the momentum of the labor in motion. Let the ball be off-center and retain the most momentum possible. A spare is easier to handle than a split between two pins on opposite sides of the alley.

Human enthusiasm is a lot like momentum. If you keep correcting it until it's heading in the right direction, the ball loses momentum. The wrong direction with a lot of enthusiasm will produce better results than a constant change of direction that diminishes enthusiasm. Irrational optimists do not understand this.

In a way, enthusiasm is directly linked to the best kind of freedom in learning. Take away the freedom to learn on your own and innovation dies. True learning builds knowledge, which builds confidence. Irrational optimists never stop changing direction. This alone is a good reason to fire them.

When we direct people, we have to avoid destroying their enthusiasm, because there's no guarantee that our direction is perfect. Even if it seems like a good idea to change direction, that act will douse the fire of enthusiasm. The only time to douse the fire is if it is out of control, dangerous, or costly. Sound leaders know this better than most. Poor leaders need to control everything—and that's fundamentally irrational.

A business client gave a job to three of his staff. The job took over fourteen months of labor, and even then they were still not done. I visited each member, and the problem surfaced right away—not one of them wanted to work to get something done, *and* they were using outdated technology. The same project was built and completed in less than two weeks with a well-known third-party service provider. When the in-house staff team visited for a meeting, the team leader spent all his time making the owner feel good about his decisions. He was a fake optimist who staged himself in such a way to make the intimidating owner feel good about what he wanted. Meanwhile, I was combative, argumentative, and firm in my stance that "these guys are wasting your time and money."

The owner accepted the completed project but he still called on the failing team for help. He needed to feel empowered—and I needed to get something done. This is not healthy, and yet we build bureaucracies through enabling relationships that promote controls rather than follow-through enthusiasm.

When an irrational optimist runs an organization, something interesting happens. The real fighters leave and the pretenders increase their control in the name of non-productive devotion. They all should be fired. Their irrational gusto eventually relies upon looking and sounding like they are working. People accepting the controller's demands feed his ego while gradually limiting individual momentum. You can recognize these political gridlocks when they maintain the status quo. Nothing great comes about because old patterns are used to protect laziness of intent.

Irrational optimists are destructive forces to all-natural momentum. We call them irrational because they pretend to stand for rational thinking. Consider such statements as "Let's have an open meeting about this," or "Let's get the others involved." These and other comments are often used to indicate honest intent, but they give everyone a chance to politicize the situation through majority manipulation and not involved consent.

Instead of the group becoming a forum to discuss policies, values, and inspire individual responsibility, the group preserves the status quo by inflating its authority with more and more controls. They thwart individual enthusiasm by maintaining diminished efficiency. Welcome to the gross negligence of fake optimism, a majority rule acquired by bottom-up idol worship of one control freak in charge! Shift that model by empowering dissenting views with real teeth in giving consent, and you will give birth to natural enthusiasm again.

The Majority Rule Manipulators

A majority decision can easily snuff out innovative dissent because most of us desire magic over responsibility. This is the number-one killer of innovation and the killer of sustainable value creation in business, religion, education, and government. If the center of leadership in any organization is not pushing for the highest level of consent while preserving common dissent in each person, then you're looking at an irrational optimist. No CEO and no board of directors will ever have the full vision and implementation needed for a company, and it is foolish to empower them with it.

More often than not, managers destroy individual momentum through group members aspiring for approval and from those with no momentum of their own. It's their very openness (without sustained vision and without allowing for dissent) that displays their fake optimism. Unlike the intimidator who abhors open gatherings, the irrational optimist thrives on the irrationalism he can pontificate free of dissent.

Follow the idolatry people shower on those in power and not the money. It is the best way to spot an organization or culture in decline.

Let's explain this problem of idolatry using the popular philosophy behind the law of attraction, also known as *The Secret*.[1] According to *The Secret*, a person's thoughts attract corresponding positive and negative life influences. The law of attraction says, "if you think it, it will materialize." Many proponents of the idea claim that, with practice, a person can use the law of attraction to manifest changes in their lives.

However, this idea has no requirement of virtue. It demands no social responsibility and allows for constant change, something irrational optimists love because it allows them to let go of difficult responsibilities in favor of a new direction with less responsibility.

This is why *The Secret* sells so well, and why new trends in cognitive manifestation and the new consciousness accession craze are so popular. It is truly hard to argue against ideas when they are spoken with high energy while offering an escape from the hard life. There is only one way to deal with these ideas. Simply ask, "How do you scale that?"

A female student gave a speech on her support of *The Secret* in my class. When she completed her ten-minute presentation, I said: "I am intoxicated with your enthusiasm but not with your idea."

By completely removing so-called negative mindsets simply wanting to ask a question, there remains no responsibility to hear any real dissent. In other words, take away social and even personal responsibility, and the majority will buy it. This can happen for only so long before society collapses, and businesses fail. This is the problem with "The Secret." It is used to avoid dissenting questions because they are deemed negative. Again, ask a motivational guru promoting the newest power hour, "How do you scale it." Invariably he will have no answers or he will call you a negative person.

When you ask how to scale something, you are essentially asking how to duplicate success. The self-improvement speaker is not you and you are not her. If there are strategies and defined processes, real systems to put in place, then fine, listen, learn, and adopt. But if it's an attitude or a certain way of being, she is not you and you are not her. Fire this person.

Irrational optimists push everything into the magical, unseen, and unknowable, always relative to themselves only. Intoxicated with their success as if it is obvious and easy for all, they will never open themselves to divergent steps and alternative principles from a wider field of agreement. If they did, they would diminish their greatness.

This doesn't negate the importance of positive thought or good mental practices, or even a great coach. It just means that the real motive remains buried, which is why you cannot debate irrational optimists by saying no. They take dissent as negative—when in fact it's more positive than magical systems that destroy individual momentum.

The problem is not just with followers of the secret; it's with fastidious religious practices, fundamentalist traditions, and even a belief in capitalism without social responsibility. No matter a person's religion, education, or economic status, no behavior or practice can replace the active movement of responsibility. A ritual doesn't replace the work of responsible faith, and capitalism doesn't guarantee a free market for all. And yet, to an irrational optimist, they do.

The point is that when the capacity of irrational optimists is tested, they elude with red herrings and return with loaded questions instead of answers. They stand toe-to-toe but not eye-to-eye. They face the fire, it seems, but without getting warm. Their motive is social worship. The only way to recognize the irrational optimist is first to have within you an intelligent concern for taking responsibility by adding value. As Samuel Dael explains in *The Christian Folly,* the suffix: "*th*" in both *faith* and *believeth* are linguistic calls to action.

A simple belief in something mimics religious salvation without the action of doing something good. It makes sense to give better groundwork to the inherent nature of faith, for faith, as we will find, is the antithesis to denial, which does not foster any responsible action.

Faith vs. Magic

Many young people apply to universities far from home. With no idea how to pay for their educations, they mail the acceptance letter and two weeks before school starts, they pack their car and head off to college.

In my case, I headed north on the Pacific Coast Highway in California. I only had $400 in my pocket, no job, and no place to stay. The year was 1991. Many students do the same every year and they are further burdened by debt before they arrive. With all this uncertainty in my own life, I knew one thing. I knew that I could find a job somewhere and that I could sleep in the pickup if needed.

Even though it takes a few days, a new student in a foreign town finds a place to call home. Maybe a job follows a month later. Until that time, many students call back home a few times in fear and panic, but because of the persistent application of effort toward what needs to be done in an uncertain situation, the tough times pass and things work out.

Even though we feel overwhelmed with fear, we exercise faith in right action. If *The Secret* had taught this, then it would have been far more popular with dissenting minds demanding deeper understanding. Irrational ideas distort faith and replace it with a desire for magic by using self-imposed positive mental exertions instead of responsible action. The proper definition of faith means *to believe*, which means thinking plus "th" meaning activity. Modern English has lost the meaning of faith. Positive thinking is not, and never will be *faith*. The best kind of positive thinking is the kind that removes mental blocks, false beliefs, general assumptions and cognitive programs that never lead to healthy action. And the only way to remove these is through responsible motion despite our fear. If done by any other means, we are stuck with just another sophisticated denial.

Too often, we anticipate a divine influence or magic solution without any work on our part. Faith is work because the universe doesn't tell us everything we need to know. If it told us everything, faith wouldn't be work, and we would not learn to think for ourselves. However, irrational optimists control how we think by telling us everything. They take from us the personal investment to exercise our mind. Just as faith without work is dead, so also is intelligence without thought dead.

We can too easily imagine that faith defies intelligence, arguing that faith is a spontaneous feeling, or supernatural energy, or the taking of a blind leap that cannot be understood. This is false and irrational. Questioning, reasoning, listening, and choosing are acts of intelligence. If intelligence doesn't perform these basic acts, it doesn't act for itself. This is why faith is best defined as a responsible action. If you are not actively compassionate, actively kind, or actively hardworking, and actively a defender of the innocent, you have no faith in the responsible action of these values. When you follow the idolatry for authority and not the money trail, you are left with one single truth: you never see responsible action in the worship of authority. This is a major clue for revealing fake people.

Let's ask a simple question. Can you exercise faith in something that is not true? If you say yes, then faith is a word with pliable meaning accessible to both the fanatic despot and the care-giving neighbor. Faith isn't neutral in this sense, as the law of attraction would like it to be. Faith has traditionally stood for adding value to the lives of others. Even though the dictionary does not say this, faith is more like an active verb than a static noun. It's an expression of virtue and not malice, and therefore it cannot be neutral to the abuse of an extremist or hidden in meaning to the most simple of hearts.

Faith must stand for the active exercise of what we know is good and true. If not, it carries little weight of value.

Irrational optimists refuse this kind of logic in applying responsible action to faith. They prefer the rhetoric of a revivalist convention to the actions of someone like Gandhi choosing to sew his own clothing in protest against foreign control of national independence.

Faith is the applied action of taking responsibility both personally and socially. This is how you can see irrational optimists. They take no personal or social responsibility for adding value. If they do, it's a token gift hoping for the social reward of acceptance. Again, follow the idolatry by seeing the authority people seek in place of taking responsible action.

Those who don't believe in magic or don't understand faith tend to adopt principles of control. Such is the view of an irrational control freak.

Imagine that a student asks a teacher a question. The teacher answers. The student returns the next day and asks more questions and the teacher offers more answers. This continues for weeks; the student asks and the teacher answers. At some point, however, the teacher should feel concerned that the student has no answers—but, instead, the teacher sits in total possession of the student's mind. The teacher has attracted what is programmed into the student.

Irrational optimists are like this teacher. They are platonic in their need for authority over others. No matter how sugar-coated their language, all energy returns to them. Seduced by their passion, irrational optimists appear to be the most open and the most approachable of all people. In truth, they are the most closed.

There are two natures in fake personalities that are hallmarks of irrational optimism. The first is being open to what they will hear but closed to what they will speak (the leftist). The second is being open to what they will speak but closed to what they will hear (the closed conservative). Both are linear and irrational; they never relate with others, especially those who are liberal in giving more access, or those who conserve value. In another book, *The High Road: Path to the Coming Renaissance*, I talk about the full breakdown of politicized and even weaponized optimism and showcase what is to come.

For a leftist not to say what he or she thinks is simply disingenuous. And a conservative's closed-mindedness in hearing other ideas is an assumption of infallibility. Irrational optimists are both. They are open about their form of magic but closed to the inclusion of any honest faith. They keep the power of both yes and no to themselves. They show great fear with absolutely no faith in the agency of others.

More Clarity

Too often in a book of this kind, we are pressed to remember various classifications and categories, types of happiness, or new verbiage on character brands that are common logic but not necessarily common to our language. Very few ideas broken into labels and categories actually stick, unless kept to just a few, and even these lose their significance over time. It seems that while labels tend to mystify, more clarity needs to surface.

Many recall in college or high school learning about the use of id, ego, and superego; type A and type B personalities; the color code; and the conscious and unconscious minds. Aristotle talked about three types of government—a monarchy (rule by one), aristocracy (rule by few), and democracy (rule by many). John Stuart Mill came up with one category of utilitarianism—the greatest good for the greatest number.

Sometimes we can't get by without breaking human action into categories, and sometimes we can. When the diagnosis of bipolar disorder came out, it gave us a name for certain behaviors, providing limited insight into human intelligence and human fear. Attention-deficit disorder is another branding without insight into clear meaning. In other words, without an accurate definition of intelligence to account for the various thinking patterns in these new terms, what we call attention deficit may be nothing but the long patience of building a concept of what is experienced in life. This would explain why some labeled as dyslexic in their youth eventually accomplish great things later in life, due to their conceptual minds eventually becoming rich enough to accommodate a greater relational capacity. This is something linguistic and linear minds fail to achieve.

A student's attention often drifts in class and reading, but we cannot call this a disorder. When we see a traumatic crash on the freeway, we all rubberneck to see the damage and continue driving for miles afterward without being alert to the road ahead. Is this a disorder?

It's the same problem with speed-readers who bullet through a book with swiftness but seem to lack the conversational experience that requires several moments of pause through the book. We can speed-read many written works. However, what do we miss with a book like the Bible or Shakespeare's Hamlet? Can a speed-reader comprehend all books without a single question that demands the mind to pause and consider the meaning of what took years for the writer to compile?

With all its hype, speed-reading is strictly linear. It doesn't produce relational meaning. It doesn't allow the mind to question while reading. This may just be a problem with slow learners. We call them disabled or dyslexia to explain away an assumed dysfunction. Why do I mention this? The irrational optimist speed-reads human beings, books, and his own mind without any relational skills. No time is given to clear away the cobwebs and remove the dust to find true meaning. Assumptions are taken on face value.

An older couple in town teaches a speed-reading class together. At one of their classes, a few questions surfaced about the meaning of a book, content about God, love, freedom, and education. They became extremely uncomfortable and quickly became intimidating optimists by avoiding the conversation. They redirected the class to move along. This is the behavior of two people who read about ten books a week. A humanities professor in town swears that speed-reading is essential to learning. In his blog posts, although clear and concise, he says very little concerning other ideas outside his field of study. When you speed-read, you think through things the same way. Everything is linear and not relational. You fail to gain insight because you have put the power of dissent and reflective questioning to the side.

Consider the following divisions of intelligence that may help you understand the concept of linear versus relational minds. At one extreme is the conceptual process; at the other is linguistic memory. Conceptual minds are more relational; linguistic minds are more linear.

Compare a vast graphics program taking up most of the computer's memory to that of a small calculating program taking up very little memory. The graphics program is slow while the calculating program operates at a very high speed. Adding memory seems to help both extremes. However, high memory intelligence with a small, fast calculating program fares better in school. It does well because it has a greater capacity for recollection. The conceptual mind has something just as important, the processing of a program such as the interrelationship of one abstract idea to another abstract idea, which responds more slowly.

Most educators teach against a student's memory rather than against a student's relational understanding. Memory and programs take up part of the total intelligence. A memory preserves and records data; a program processes that data.

A conceptual intelligence (more program than memory) has a hard time retaining data because it is trying to process as it goes. These minds often appear slow and those possessing them have many questions. They may even have difficulty phrasing the questions, especially if their thoughts are drifting to process new information.

This is a genuine optimist in embryo. The tendency to use the term "attention deficit" does them no justice. Younger minds may appear almost void of memory and this may highlight their behavioral distractions even more. Over time, however, they eventually learn to relate to concepts and people because they have taken the time to pause and consider meanings and connections. We may label them in their youth, but in their adult years, they build a life program that yields insight and wisdom.

Irrational optimists aren't like this. They relate to very little and rarely acquire the wisdom they pretend to have. They are all memory with no conceptual whole.

The Point

Relational intelligence builds over years of mental processing; it might even become faster in time than the immediate recall of memory. This is the great secret the irrational optimist never understands. Have you ever seen a fast calculating mind in its youth become full of wisdom in later years? Take even a child prodigy, do you ever hear of such a gifted person accomplishing great things later in their life? There's a great richness of humanity in an older and more conceptual mind compared to a youthful and purely linguistic one.

This is essentially the difference between relational and linear thinking. Collecting data records will never secure the desired meaning. The rare exception is the occasional genius like Shakespeare, showing both linear recall in using a vast vocabulary and a relational insight revealing the dynamic connection of each word employed.

Many researchers have established similar distinctions: between left and right brains, between yin and yang, between romantic and classic. You can have all the reference data in your head, such as categories, types, and classifications, but without a relational concept pulled from many sources and sifted through a lot of discussions, you find yourself unable to relate.

Are we not found wanting as a society in this regard? This is the basic problem with irrational optimists: they remain stuck in their limited range obtained without discussion and debate. They reach far in their minds for a single view, but they never turn their heads for a second or third view. This makes for terrible and destructive leadership. They should be fired because they can misdirect an entire organization far off course.

If you could point to one good thing our education system has destroyed, here it is. We favor linear thinking over relational connections. We kill the oral traditions of "no" in favor of a contrived and forced lecture of "yes." We are educated without meaning and we speed-read without developing sound questions. We live without the internal pause of a personal conversation.

The first time I realized this problem came while reading Herman Melville's *Moby-Dick*. It was the scene in the book where Starbuck, the first mate, challenged Captain Ahab. Starbuck said something revealing on the quarterdeck for the other mates to hear: "Captain Ahab, I have heard of Moby-Dick—but it was not Moby-Dick that took off thy leg?" The captain then said in a whipped reply, "Who told thee that?"

At this point, I couldn't read any further. For days, I thought about the implication of this scene while the rest of the class continued reading the book. I thought, if Moby-Dick had nothing to do with taking Ahab's leg, then why does the captain blame the whale? What was the captain's problem? At the same time I was reading, *The Denial of Death* by Ernest Becker and he answered the question. The whale was a scapegoat for Ahab's denial of death. By killing the whale, he sought to repress his fear of mortality, at least in his own mind. Ahab's problem became a symbolic one. Ahab was trying to kill death.

It took about two weeks to fully wrap my mind around this concept. By the time I was fully aware of the new understanding, the rest of the class had moved on. I was left behind in the class but far ahead in life. I started to read all great literature with a pressing sense of mortality.

A conceptual understanding is not the sum of human experience. It is a sense of responsible meaning that helps connect life experience to other thoughts. Irrational optimists streamline any conceptual abilities to avoid responsibility and they shift that into a magical escape. While a conceptual mind struggles to make sense of bits of data by placing the details into a larger whole; the linear mind can file data with very little order. To a genuine optimist, this seems irrational.

A friend had to pass a state contractor's test. He memorized the answers to the test and passed without understanding the relevant meaning. The conceptual mind struggles to file things away until it can fit the same into a larger context. That larger context is a way of seeing things from a broader perspective.

Another good friend prepared to take the same exam and instead of plowing through the test with the least amount of effort and with no meaning, he decided to spend a good year studying several books on new green building technologies to get a bigger picture for himself. He even attended several construction sites to take part in building homes using a solar, radiant barrier, insulated concrete forms, and geothermal technologies.

This second behavior makes for great doctors, lawyers, teachers and practitioners in many fields. They have the bedside quality that can reach across with a depth of meaning to add character to their vast and detailed knowledge. You will never see this range of understanding with irrational optimists because they don't think relationally. The only way to see the emptiness in the irrational optimist is if you get more responsible meaning in yourself.

Holding fast to the responsible action to key words is the enemy of fake optimism, especially irrational optimists. Take the word *love* as a simple example. Is it just a feeling or is it an action? If it is just a feeling, it can be anything with no responsible action required. The irrational optimist will buy into this idea with almost no hesitation. However, if love requires some action, at least all can see and agree to action being a primary base to build on. Then, when we see the action, we verify the meaning to be true. We cannot verify something that is in your head. Irrational optimists keep as much in their head as possible.

Making sure all can see responsible action connected to the words listed below is called the conservation of meaning. We preserve the true action of a word where all can see the meaning, rather than pontificate a meaning with no actionable equivalent.

It is out of a struggle for rich and well-defined words (obtained through open consent) that we can stand against all fake optimists.

Take a moment to think about key abstract nouns used in a discussion, such as those listed below. Try to find their responsible application and then open yourself to dialogue with others. If a responsible action (both individually and socially) is avoided or disregarded in a conversation, you know the other person is fake and irrational.

You are welcome to add to the list. Therapeutically open discussion of these words in business, family, and community life will increase responsibility and decrease contradiction that too often surfaces in the escape of a staged optimist, the control of an intimidator, and the magic plagued by the irrational mind.

Angels	Economics
Art/Beauty	Electric
Being/Existence	Evolution
Belief	Emotion
Brotherhood	Energy
Capitalism	Enterprise
Causality/Infinity	Epistemology
Chance	Equality
Charity/Service	Ethics
Citizen	Evil
Communication	Evolution
Community	Faith
Conservation	Family
Conservatism	Fear
Constitution	Federalism
Culture	Form/Law
Currency	Freedom/Free Will
Death/Life	Friendship
Deduction	Globalism
Definition	God
Democracy	Government
Denial	Health
Desire	Heaven
Distinction	Hell
Dream	History
Duty/Responsibility	Hope

Hypothesis
Ideal
Imagination
Induction
Intelligence/IQ
Interpretation
Joy
Justice/Judgment
Knowledge
Leadership
Learning/Education
Liberalism
Liberty
Light
Love
Magnetic
Marriage/Family
Meaning
Media
Medicine
Memory
Metaphysics
Monarchy
Moral
Morality
Myth
Nature
Nutrition
Obedience
Opposition
Optimism
Ownership/Georgics
Philosophy
Physics
Politics
Principle

Prophecy
Providence
Psychology/ Psychiatry
Quality
Reason/Logic
Relativity
Responsibility
Revelation
Revolution
Rhetoric
Righteousness
Rights
Sacrifice
Science
Sin
Socialism
Sovereignty
Soul
Space
Spirit/Spiritual
Sport
State
Statesmanship
Taxation
Technology
Terror/Intimidation
Time
Tradition
Truth
Tyranny
Value
Vice
Virtue
War
Wealth
Wisdom

The best existential analysis of the human condition leads directly into the problems of God and faith.

Ernest Becker, The Denial of Death

Faith is the highest passion in a human being. Many in every generation may not come that far, but none comes further.

Soren Kierkegaard

4
The Believing Optimist

In belief lies the secret of all valuable exertion
-Bulwer

This is Work

Many say that optimism is simply an attitude of mind—a state of carrying a positive outlook. If so, then why not use other synonyms for attitude and place "positive" in front of each? These synonyms include a *positive boldness*, a *positive brashness*, a *positive arrogance*, a *positive assertion* and perhaps *positive defiance*.

Each one of these can have both positive and negative connotations. Our mistake comes from thinking that one's positivity is always good and that it never has dark aspirations. We see the same with most personality profiles. Have you ever taken a personality test that revealed a negative profile? They are all somewhat positive. Perhaps human beings are best seen in a good light when they are alone. However, the minute we organize into a hierarchy of power, personality profiles change, sometimes drastically. Thus far, we have talked of three fake optimists to uncover this very problem.

If we look at optimism as having two sides, we see that it either aligns with the drive to control and take away value (fake), or it becomes one's drive to add value (genuine). The latter requires some work. The former may be the ultimate condition of the devil.

It is easy to say, "I'm an eternal optimist." It is *work* to say, "I never give up on a good thing." The eternal optimist can be fake. He can be a staged personality, a smiling intimidator, or an irrational peddler of magic. None of these show any work that supports their optimism. Their claim as optimists comes, rather, from an inner desire to control. It's like gathering crops to sell that were planted by someone else. When the fall season arrives and it's time to gather the crops, it is easy to focus on your reward and preach to others of your success. Meaning, it's easy to be an eternal optimist if what you harvest takes from the work of another man or woman. There is a big difference between what you reap and what you sow. Fake optimists focus on what they reap. Genuine optimists attend to what they sow.

Fake optimists live for immediate transactions. Genuine optimists seek the past, present, and future.

Have you ever met a person so busy making money or climbing a political ladder that he doesn't add value? He figures out how to get a bigger piece of the action, or more control, without adding value of their own. We look on him as a success and we think, "He's optimistic." He even stands in front of us at a chamber of commerce luncheon and tells us how to achieve triumph while quietly telegraphing how to avoid telling the truth. Often these same people proclaim, "I'm an eternal optimist," appearing constructive without really adding anything of worth. So what is the proof we should look for to inspire genuine optimism in our own lives? Who are the people we should hire to replace the fake ones we have just fired?

You might be surprised.

In times of great difficulty, those who say, "I refuse to give up on a good thing," are certainly optimistic. We could also call them full of faith. The way you can tell for sure is when someone suffers to protect the truth.

In American history, the only death by *peine forte et dure* (pressing to death) was performed on Giles Corey, who was pressed to death on September 19, 1692, during the Salem witch trials. Because he refused to enter a plea after being accused of being a witch in the judicial proceeding, his last words, according to legend, were, "More weight." This may sound extraordinary, but it's the source of strength of genuine optimism and real faith.

Genuine optimism rises from the will to take on *more* weight and *more* responsibility, rather than find a way to escape. Fake optimists, by way of contrast, justify their escape in an attempt to save their image.

The proof we need doesn't come from someone saying he believes in something. Merely asserting a belief has an ingredient missing because a mental belief alone lacks the substance of faith. The real substance becomes a worthy sacrifice.

Attached to the belief, as correctly stated by the 18th-century writer Edward Bulwer-Lytton, "valuable exertion" illustrates a connection between the sowing and the reaping.

Of all genuine optimists, *believing* optimists sow their worthy effort in a very pragmatic way. You can feel and see their optimism in live-action rather than through verbal assertion. Hire them before someone else does because believing optimists are willing to take on more weight. They are hard workers. They possess that extra ingredient that manifests their trust in our agency. Trust is a great synonym for faith, and you can trust believing optimists. Hire them now!

Like Chuck

Chuck Stamps is an example of a believing optimist. A retired cook from the US Coast Guard, Chuck is a broad-shouldered man who loves to give hugs. No matter how much taller you are, he somehow wraps his arms around your neck and lifts his eyes level with yours. Believing optimists have this quality. Their concern is what they do for another, in how they make you feel, and in how they add warmth and service to your life. To debate over principle is unproductive, and to encourage any right action from someone else is not their focus.

To many people, optimism is a belief that the existing world is the best possible world. For the believing optimist, the thought is extended to ask, why worry and why get frustrated trying to understand motive and principle? All that matters is the good you can do.

Another definition holds that optimism is a belief that good always prevails.

Both fit the nature of a believing optimist. They don't see evil, not because they *avoid* it, but because they stay focused on the good they can achieve on their own.

The staged optimist covers his evil intent in performance and never accomplishes the good he professes to want. A believing optimist accomplishes good in the most direct way possible. He just does it.

Here's an example of what I'm talking about. Chuck helped single moms and college students away from home. On Mondays he cooked dinner at a local church for hungry college students attending Humboldt State University in the redwoods of Northern California, all on his own dime and with the help of a local produce distributor and several grocery stores.

A true believing optimist's motive comes from a fundamental principle of "doing good," and this is what sets him apart. He lives to touch lives—versus the staged optimist who lives to get attention without touching anyone.

A simple philosophy of life goes something like this: add more value than you take and do this for as long as you can. Some people aren't able to give to their communities because of illness, disability, or other handicaps; this is why more is required from those who can. At some point, we all need to take from the community—but not everyone at the same time. It would surprise most of us how easy it is to add value, even with extreme disabilities. A believing optimist sees this better than most.

For example, I met a woman at a title agency who had to leave work for thirty minutes to go home and turn her bedridden husband to avoid bedsores. Before a recent injury causing him to be bedridden, he'd been independently mobile and could make his way to the family-owned auto repair shop in his electric chair and help diagnose mechanical problems. Even though he was a quadriplegic, with the help of a voice-activated computer he maintained the accounting, paid invoices, and managed information flow.

You could see this woman talk about her husband with deep love, despite his disabilities and what she had to do for him every day. This is exactly what believing optimists do: they touch others' hearts by bringing out the best of themselves. Everything they do comes from a deep-seated drive to touch lives with the best that they are.

The unique attribute about believing optimists is that they trade the distant stage for real human connections. The disabled husband is a life-force magnet from whom many people seek advice and friendship. Without the ability to move his arms and legs, he adds a massive degree of value. He's a believing optimist; he must add something to the world, to his family, to his immediate contacts, and others. Staged optimists add nothing.

What good is the world if we cannot add the best of what we have? This is the fundamental drive of believing optimists. They may not know their underlying principles, and they may not encourage others to perform any right action as much as they give of themselves. The nature of what they give is the rich stuff called intimacy, the very opposite of what's seen in the staged performer.

Staged optimists are unable to undress themselves on stage and reveal their hearts. Believing optimists do it naturally. Unlike staged optimists who lift themselves above others, believing optimists lower themselves below others. Christ-like people are believing optimists. They descend below them all.

Today many people add value through teaching children the principle of persistence, setting an example of giving to those in need, and still, they can build relationships, fire-new enterprises, launch new technologies, and create new organizational models with more freedom and less central control.

From the Inside

Believing optimists add value from inside. Their value comes in acts of patience, of long-suffering, of gentleness and kindness to others, rather than leadership qualities like encouragement or the innovative value of advancing knowledge and principle. We'll see both qualities in other genuine optimists. Believing optimists aren't prone to becoming leaders in a political world, yet they are the first to step out to lead and take responsibility.

Believing optimists are perfect examples of adding value since the value to them advances charity and builds character without hypocrisy. They are the real-life manifestation of everything we value in a friend. They judge nobody, and even though they may hold strong religious doctrines and beliefs, they never deny you the expression of your own mind. There can be no greater value than the support of another person's freedom. Just look at how believing optimists have faith in self. They also show great self-motivation and their reward is self-realization. See **Figure 4-1.**

Fig. 4–1 Traits of the Beieiving Optimist

Character	Traites
Idolatry	Faith in Self
Intelligence	Glory in Being
Agency	Obeys Truth
Motivation	Self Motivation
Reward	Self Realization

Too often we think of value as a physical product or something of monetary worth. Value isn't something in the market. Value is the action that replenishes and improves, the real stuff from the inside. Whether this action is through upholding a principle, or giving a service, or motivating a team, all genuine optimists—especially believing optimists—hold one thing most true, that optimism is not the attitude you portray but the actions that match the attitude.

Sometimes this action exhibits more kindness, more encouragement, or a firm stand of *no* to force a principled *yes*. While staged optimists place the return of value to the self; believing optimists place the return of value to the community, the family, and friends. They see the connection to the inside of others more valuable than a return of value to their self.

Just the other day my daughter ignited a discussion when a family member made her feel bad. A comment followed from my observation,

> Some think in very straight lines and only for themselves. They are linear. Then some include others in their thoughts. They are relational. Every time you think of doing something, consider how it affects everyone you can, the family, friends, and neighbors, even the homeless. You will build stronger relations with others if you practice this.

By directly giving value to one's immediate community, this same value conserves its energy and returns seven times greater. This is the opposite of a staged optimist who talks big about helping but never suggests how we can help each other. Staged optimists are like a fake politician because they never show any real human touch. The believing optimist can never exist in politics because this person needs too much real intimate touch. Oddly, this is what makes for a better leader, because it is real and not fake. If we could do one thing to improve our world, we should find a way to get more believing optimists into leadership positions.

The modern religious or political zealot is a negative example of a believing optimist. You see the same thing with self-help trends in forced positive thinking. They put on a great act, trying to be close, but they refuse to take the step toward greater enlightenment. If you were to ask a believing optimist what it means to believe in something, this person would say, "What I do to the least in my community I do to me." This is exactly how believing optimists live their life. They show concern for those at the bottom of despair and they focus on what they can do to help. There can be no better meaning of belief. Anyone who disagrees is not his brother's keeper.

Key to Character

Believing optimists seldom fret over peripheral issues of tradition and authority. They are more concerned with the central issue of serving a need and not telling people what to believe. Fundamentalists waiting for a magical rapture to come out of the skies and save them will never make "serving others" the true rapture. On the other hand, a believing optimist will.

Believing optimists connect with people and make lasting friendships because they listen and are willing to put out a hand to help another. For fake optimists, this is not enough. To believing optimists, it's more than enough because it defines their character concerning their community.

Believing optimists preserve the powers of free agency, whereas fundamentalists and evangelists or any academic know-it-all too often want to counsel you, just like self-help gurus telling you how upbeat they are without feeling the beating of your heart. Neither the evangelist nor the motivational guru has a clue as to what is in your mind or your heart.

Years ago while standing outside a movie theater in Brentwood California, a young Christian evangelist approached me with zeal and said, "You live in sin until you accept the blood and sacrifice of Christ our Savior." A believing optimist sees through all this as coercion on the part of an intruding enthusiast. Rather than focus on physical images such as the virgin birth or blood sacrifice of Christ's death, believing optimists look instead at mimicking Christ's life. They then lead exemplary lives or they take on Thoreau's philosophy of peaceful dissent. Compare that to modern safe spaces on campuses that are not safe at all. They are constrictions of dissent.

Two Powers

A lot of religious fanaticism and political rhetoric looks and feels like believing optimism, but in truth, they're staged optimists willing to get in your face and never in your heart. The best way to see the genuine apart from the staged is to measure how well gurus of goodness support your two powers of free agency.

For example, do they openly and willingly support your free agency to dissent? And do they support the same free agency to consent? If they are bothered with your twin powers of freedom (to say no and yes), then you know they are staged and political in their optimism.

Believing optimists don't ask questions of meaning as would an encouraging optimist and they don't stand up in dissent of self-evident principles. They just allow total freedom to speak. The atmosphere of a believing optimist is like group therapy. While there might exist an adversarial relationship in the group, believing optimists are the last to judge and the first to touch. Believing optimists will always believe in your best potential, even when you've failed to show your best effort. At the bottom of any trial in life, even at the bottom step of shame, believing optimists will be the first to descend and be there for you.

In 1983, volunteers arrived to help sandbag the dam of a local reservoir after heavy snow in the mountains caused flooding when the temperatures rose. We worked hard to prevent damage to the pristine campgrounds, the golf shop, the park ranger's station, and the newly seeded cornfields below the dam.

I was an 80-pound 10-year-old and unable to lift the 50-pound bags. An older girl handed me a shovel and showed me how to fill the bags with sand. A great urgency filled the night and everyone pitched in: the task belonged to all. One farmer arrived with extra shovels in his truck and another brought a tractor with a front loader. It took most of the night to patch things up under the light of a warm full moon.

This experience is similar to many events we read about in history. Consider the night of March 4, 1776, when General John Thomas and 2,000 troops marched to the top of Dorchester Heights in Boston. During the night, they hauled fortifications behind bales of hay (placed between the path taken by the troops and the harbor) to muffle their movements. These troops hauled and placed earthworks and cannons. General Washington provided moral support in the early morning hours of what was the sixth anniversary of the Boston Massacre. By dawn, fortifications had been constructed, including barrels filled with rocks that could be rolled down the hill at attacking troops.

The amazing thing about this event is how much was accomplished by so few and in just one single night. This is how powerful believing optimism can fill the air: it brings out the best in everyone because there is an applied faith accessible to all. Fake optimists never give others that kind of belonging because they separate themselves as elitists.

Many self-help writers have assisted with individual needs and have given solace to many people. What they don't show is a certain discrepancy between how they look in the mirror but disregard the lives around them. The best ideas generally focus on value-adding action and not on cognitive mirrors. Don't get confused. Higher frequency thinking leading to greater freedom of mind is always important, but if your internal spirit doesn't match a similar action in living, something's wrong.

This is where a lot of motivational talk misses the mark. It also explains why we need the external optimism of social responsibility to fire up personal responsibility toward adding greater value. We need the two powers of yes and no in perfect companionship at all times. When we learn to scale these two powers that everyone has into greater social responsibility, we become a believing culture of optimism once again.

Too much self-help and religious motivation does it from the individual's point of view without interacting with others. This is why believing optimists are so important: they have to make real connections with others or they simply cannot take part. They are the first to manifest outwardly the good inside their hearts. They are purely relational in how they need to touch others. This is opposite of the staged optimist who is removed from the needs of others. When the situation turns political, believing optimists are the first to step away because they have no stomach for compulsory imperatives.

This explains why fake optimists have gained control over others' free agency: they always demand more control so they can force consent while believing optimists back off from using force.

Make no mistake, the need for motivation is very important. Nobody likes a sourpuss in the office in the home. A negative cloud lacks productivity and too often inhibits building relations with others. Even worse, very few people can endure listening to fear-laden problems day in and day out. Such a person can take more from the company, more from family members, and more from the community than they give.

Even with that said, at times, the expression of personal fear in an open setting is needed to share compassion and sentiment. Open expression of the unsettled heart helps us all to see a reason for the fear. If we don't allow free expression to work through issues that might otherwise fester, issues often develop into emotional disabilities, triggered senses, and eventually into denial.

When political, religious, and motivational tools of denial cover genuine fear, we have a serious problem: we'll never be challenged to correct ourselves.

This problem surfaces with linear minds that employ denial. They inhibit relational minds from challenging their motives. More knowledge of how linear minds and relational minds approach life is helpful.

Linear Versus Relational

Take Shakespeare's *Hamlet* as a fascinating example of linear versus relational thinking. Imagine the ghost of your father suddenly appearing to you in the wet damp of a foggy night. Imagine also that the ghostly figure of your dead father reveals to you his premature death and murder by the hand of his brother, your uncle. Finally, imagine that your uncle is married to your mother and it has only been a month since the death of your father. Would this eerie experience cause you to behave crazily?

Add to this a liberal education in the classics, as Hamlet had, and you compound the experience with insights gained from philosophy, art, history, and poetry, all of which Hamlet used as intellectual weaponry for avoiding the responsibility to avenge his father's murder.

Yes, it's true, reading classics can give you greater relational depth. Sadly, if studied alone, without the oral tradition that infuses responsibility into human character through question-and-answer discussion, reading the classics is more debilitating and linear. This is worse for speed-readers who refuse open discussion of what they read.

Affected with overwhelming knowledge, Hamlet's condition near the end of the play states, "I am dead." Optimism must be made of much sterner stuff than this. It's not good when we seem affected by the darkest realities of life without optimism that sees through great challenges. Socrates, Christ, Martin Luther King Jr., and many others teach that moving forward through massive opposition is not impossible. Just look at self-absorbed artists who take their lives while great leaders sacrifice their lives. Those willing to take on "more weight" in life show more optimism.

Hamlet expresses an attitude on the short side of optimism. The only difference is that he has the language to express his illiterate courage, which makes him such a fascinatingly trag-ic figure. Some call this madness; however, it's more accurate to call it a handicap. Unless one can make positive action that adds value, there is no real optimism, no matter how elevated one's language.

This need for positive action rests at the core of believing optimists because they must do something good they can relate. Staged optimists relate to nothing, but they do reveal their linear approach.

For instance, a person with a linear mind will see a home-less person and say, "If they can hold a sign saying 'homeless need food,' they can get a job." The person with the relational mind will walk over and talk with the homeless person to find out why they are homeless. This builds knowledge to relate to the homeless person's situation rather than passing judgment created by detached and linear conclusions. While neither is giving anything like a handout, the relational effort has a better understanding.

Fake people are linear. Genuine people are relational.

This doesn't make linear minds the filth of society. It just means that our world remains mostly governed by linear think-ing. Linear thinking favors central control at greater and greater distances. With the world controlled mostly by linear minds, we have more conclusions detached from real understanding.

Genuine optimists are not political people and central control is a serious disadvantage to them. With central control, there's no appeals process against power centers and no open free expression to dissent against power with real teeth. Most of all, there is no connection to people.

Many collapsing societies lose their relational under-standing because they become fixated on death as a linear prob-lem and they forget to live in relationship to others as a real solution to life. Just about every television show today centers on some aspect of death. Music videos plaster sunken cheeks of horror with skin and bones to match and we just love to look at the carnage of murder and death to satiate our need to feel that we are alive. Meanwhile, we have no understanding of what is motivating us.

The viewer becomes the prisoner of his fear. Because we fear life and death, we look at morbid scenes to feel alive. This is pure linear thinking. It's like the gladiators and war games held in the Coliseum in ancient Rome. The spectacle of death made the audience feel alive. To see others slaughtered makes your life suddenly seem safe from death. What a great diversion given to the people so they would not focus on the real problems of inequality and political injustice? Do we do the same in modern life as in ancient Rome?

Relational thinking says, it's true we are mortal. It also claims that we all should be a part of making this world the best of all possible worlds. Denial is a linear attempt to repress awareness of the elephant in the room. Faith sees the elephant and looks at a solution to remove problems through relational understanding that leads to greater service to others.

Today we lack genuine optimism and the necessary value-adding action to live in authentic relationships. We're worse than Hamlet. We've become the comatose face of ennui and Hamlet is slapping us in the face. At least Hamlet had the gumption to fight at the last minute for justice and die. We just keep looking in the mirror trying to find out what is wrong inside. We never realize that the problem rests not so much in the glitches in our cognitive insides or in our emotional pasts, but in failing to engage in open discussion, the very thing that liberates all genuine optimists.

Meditative Verses Purpose

If we keep thinking that we must push ourselves away from the controlling influence of others (the rugged individualism approach), and if we keep following the idolatry of authority (the zealot's approach), we are following a frozen methodology. These are linear dead ends. The first avoids building relationships and the second allows authority over our free agency.

Sometimes we can remove these two constraints through meditation, but rarely do we find our purpose and live our lives in a meditative state. This is the basic logic of believing optimists. While some genuine optimists actively live as they see within their minds, and while other genuine optimists actively live as they are inspired to lift others, the believing optimist actively lives as they feel. If they feel to do good, they are genuine optimists. If they feel to do harm and they are open about it, they are honest but not optimistic. Always remember, a genuine optimist, in keeping with the true meaning of the word, focuses on the optimal best that can happen.

If we just focus on changing our thinking to change our lives, there's no guarantee that we'll see and accept our own fear. There is no guarantee good will happen. With no effort to reach out and understand others, we escape from social responsibility in life. Believing optimists do not seek to escape life this way. Their main concern is some good they can bring to others by seeking understanding, by listening, and just by being there. They are great at letting you talk. As long as they can do something good for you, which can be as simple as saying nothing and letting your twin powers of freedom figure out a solution, they're happy.

The real difference between the linear mind and the relational mind is demonstrated in what they're willing to let inside. A forced political body assembled into a vertical organization creates power structures too far removed and too difficult for a genuine optimist to combat. Modern advertisements prove this one-way method by encouraging minds to react without question. The reaction comes through subliminal methods while we put aside our free will to disagree and question.

When we interact with other programmed minds, and when we avoid any expression of dissent, we reinforce incorrect meanings into our traditions. Without oral discussion coupled with the right to dissent, we'll never be able to eradicate authoritative controllers.

Without open access to add value, believing optimists are limited. They may challenge the staged optimist by building genuine relationships, but not when it comes to challenging intimidators or the promotion of irrational magic. This is why we have encouraging optimists to tackle the worst enemy of individual freedom, the Intimidator! If not, then we need principled optimists willing to rise in strong dissent against the magic of idolatry that comes with centralized authority.

Let's move now to the first of these two, a very powerful form of optimism we call encouragement. Outside of believing optimism, this is the first step toward a social optimism that's truly accessible to all.

5
The Encouraging Optimist

Correction does much, but encouragement does more.
Encouragement after censure is as the sun after a shower.

- Goethe

What is Encouragement?

While believing optimists measure accomplishments by bringing out the best in themselves, an encouraging optimist measures accomplishment by bringing out the best in others. The good news is that we can move from believing to encouraging. It is a natural progression. When they're together in one person, they are everyone's dream boss.

Encouragement is pretty much the opposite of intimidation, which imposes uncertainty through your own actions. Here's what's different: encouraging optimists love liberty, openness, and conversation, which brings out the best in others through a process of open consent that has both rough and smooth edges. Encouragement is not always a bed of rose petals, but it does eventually bring out the best in others.

The Rough Edges

There's often one person who encourages us to give our best. In my case, the first person that comes to mind was a college professor named Jerry Fetch. He taught courses in humanities, business, and marketing at Moorpark College in Southern California, and Jerry knew how to encourage the best out of each student.

It was late afternoon in the spring semester of 1985 and Jerry found me walking my bike away from the campus library. He called out to me and I parked the bike and joined him in his office. "Sit down," he said. "Do you mind if I make an observation?"

Sitting stiff in a hard plastic chair near the door of his modest and narrow office, I said, hesitantly, "No."

"You do not have one thing about you that is dynamic," he said, hitting dead center on my ego, like being forced to look into a mirror for the first time to see a big mole on the tip of my nose. I was speechless, hurt, and unsure of how to respond. I felt offended and waited for the hurt to go away.

At that time in my life, I was studying to be an actor, specifically a film actor. I was taking private lessons at the home of Frank Roach, an accomplished actor who also taught at the same college. I was pretty much impressed with what I was doing... and still, there was not a single thing about me that was great, and Jerry brought this realization out and into the open. While sitting in his office, I was certainly not in a safe place. I was told something I preferred to ignore.

Sometimes we need to see what we hide pushed to the outside. It is like seeing as we are seen of others, which is better than a mirror.

Jerry wasn't finished. "Instead, what you have are many qualities that, when properly aligned, create an incredible character."

For months, all I could focus on was the thought that I didn't have a single thing about me that was dynamic. It took another six months to see the truth, quit my direction in the performing arts, and get a better path of action to fill the measure of my real potential. I suspect that Jerry probably told the same thing to many students over the years.

Encouraging optimists are excellent mentors at any point in our lives. They build on the qualities of a believing optimist and compound their effect in what they pull out of you. The secret to their success is leaving your agency in place by showing faith in you, opposite of how the intimidator works. Supporting another's free will requires a certain practice of faith rarely understood by those who think that intimidation can be optimistic. Why faith? Because it's faith that demands an alert mind rather than a comatose following. For the encouraging optimist, this faith comes through a kind of tough love that has been sorely misconstrued by those who think they can practice tough love without a relational understanding.

If a relationship isn't established between two people, the practice of tough love is too easily wasted, because it will be misunderstood when it's delivered. Think about it, the word tough and love do not go together naturally. People who practice tough love, without any established relationship able to withstand the intervention, do so more out of the denial of their own fear of rejection (to look confident) than anything expressive of faith (that is confident). Consider the old adage a father says to a disobedient child before a spanking, "this is going to hurt me more than it will hurt you." Does the child feel any love in that action? How easy is the spanking misinterpreted?

Think of tough love as being tough on the one giving correction and not on the one receiving correction. This means that one must first establish a relationship of love and friendship—which takes time—before offering an observation that may be tough to express. The intimidator wants to shift tough love onto the person receiving the observation or correction. Encouraging people to take the toughness on themselves. Rather than "this is going to hurt me more than it will hurt you," it changes to "I do not want to hurt you, but can we please talk, I need to say something."

Which of the two options has a better chance of being received? Obviously the second.

The reason Jerry could make that comment is that a relationship had been built between us through my attending several of his classes over two years. This gave him the connection he needed to say something difficult and for my benefit.

We all have a friend who tries to show tough love without ever taking the time to talk or listen to us. The best relationships are those that take a long time to build. Those that are built quickly tend to suffer when it becomes clear (over time, or via a crisis) that they don't have the necessary connection.

Parents reject their children by being tough on them without taking the time to understand who their children really are. You can be tough but allow for more time to build the relationship through discussion.

For instance, encouraging optimists are very patient and are usually the first to say, "We have all the time in the world." The intimidating optimist will say, "We don't have all the time in the world." Most genuine optimists favor giving more time to decision-making. Fake optimists favor giving less time to decision-making. The challenge in reaching mutual consent and deeper connections comes in having enough freedom of discussion—and the time required—to work out differences. If there's no relationship, there is only one way to speak freely, toss everyone in a room and make them talk until they reach an agreement. Allow for debate, round table openness, heaps of discussion, and tons of mastermind bantering. It brings people closer and builds a highly functioning team of genuine optimists.

Pushed Together

A good example is the 1957 classic movie *Twelve Angry Men*, with Henry Fonda. In the movie, twelve male jurors exit the courtroom to decide the fate of a young man tried for murder. Without any deliberation, all the jurors vote for a conviction quickly except one man, Juror 8 (played by Henry Fonda), who insists on more discussion.

After many hours of debate, one juror at a time begins to see more reason to doubt what had seemed to be a slam-dunk conviction at the start. What is most interesting is the patience that was tested by every juror, especially on a hot July day with no air-conditioning. All it took was one juror to hold everything up and demand some answers to his questions of doubt. When pushed together to reach a unanimous consent, just one person alone can help eleven others overcome bigotry, racial prejudice, and apathy for justice. A rule by majority, which easily succumbs to intimidation, can never do this.

A free society is not a safe space. It is defined by anger, prejudice, and long, spitting debates in an openly adversarial environment trying to reach consent. Challenging generalized assumptions and quick impatient judgments are healthy practices because they result in better understanding.

The great lesson this movie teaches is that discussion, a lot of it, and with plenty of time to work out differences, is good. Only when we ask the attention-seekers to define their terms and reveal their facts will we eliminate the political grand-standers.

A real-life example is the organized effort of nonprivileged classes (also called the third estate) in France in 1789. The 576 deputies of this third estate represented 98% of the population. After realizing they would be outvoted by the two privileged orders, namely the clergy and the nobility, they formed their own National Assembly. Finding themselves locked out of their usual meeting hall at Versailles on June 20, 1789, and thinking that the king was forcing them to disband and go home, they moved their assembly to a nearby indoor tennis court. There they took an oath "not to separate, and to reassemble wherever circumstances require until the constitution of the kingdom is established." In the face of this much solidarity, King Louis XVI consented and on June 27 ordered the clergy and the nobility to join the third estate in the new National Assembly.

Thereafter on August 4th of that year came the Abolition of Feudalism (people separated into classes, such as monarchs, vassals, nobles, and peasants), and on August 26 The Declaration of the Rights of Man was passed. All this launched the French Revolution because a group of people refused to separate until they had an agreement. Even though the revolution turned bloody, better representation and the abolition of bad ideas eventually took hold.

In some situations, many will assume there is prejudice when there is none. However, given enough time and in close proximity (when we are pushed together), just about any prejudice can be dissolved. Fake dissenters often stand up only for attention with no desire to dissolve disagreement. This may cause many honest individuals to hold back for fear of what others might think. Only in an environment of unanimous consent and with no escape as in the examples above can we ask those looking for attention to *explain their motives, define their terms,* and *reveal their facts.* This is the power of representative democracy, a process that protects both voice and vote together and in the same room. Popular democracy removes the engaged discussion and we have no voice or expressed dissent and only a vote. Intimidating optimists remove the voice of expression and let us have a vote only, but always with the forced imperative to vote as required by the collective hierarchy.

If we could really unload what's on our minds, and relinquish what we feel in our hearts, and if we could do this without the fear of becoming marginalized, and if we had enough time and opportunity to be challenged and corrected, we could overcome and accomplish so much more as individuals and as a people. This process is exactly what defined the great oral traditions of the past, such as those that lead to the Magna Carta, the dialogues of Socrates, the debate that created a constitutional government in the United States, and even a team in any organization trying to achieve something great by letting open discussion lead the way to greater on-board consent.

Without this vigorous and "fierce conversation" about ideas and not complaints, and without taking enough time to work disagreements out, we've become a polarized people without understanding each other. This very nature of freedom has fallen and risen many times in history. It appears we are being called upon to restore it once again.

Unanimous consent (as seen in the jury process and in creating constitutional rights) removes idolatry toward certain individuals. Acting free from these powers sometimes becomes a rough road through the process, but it's the only way to reach a consensus and smooth out the edges of controversy.

Smooth Edges

The smooth edges of encouragement are the lifting quality of all optimism. You see this in open and free talk, the power found only in the encouraging optimist.

When the chips are down and a crisis is in the air, we call upon motivational inspiration to rally the masses. The problem occurs when that political motivator tells a lie. When this happens, the political liar gives an open door for our escape from responsibility to question the lie and those who dare challenge the motivator fall in battle against the new popular movement. The result is that the genuine optimism of "no" appears to be anti-optimistic. We now see the grand power of intimidating optimism; it moves the masses but never the free will of the individual. Intimidation is the direct opposite of encouragement.

The poet Ezra Pound is a good example of appearing antagonistic while in fact being encouraging. Despite his stand against Jews, and despite his support of fascism at one time, he spoke out against usury after having experienced the ravages of World War I while living in Europe. Ezra Pound was arrested in 1945 on charges of treason and incarcerated in St Elisabeth's Psychiatric hospital in Washington DC for twelve years.

Pound was against all forms of finance capitalism, which he called usury. He sided with Lenin and Hitler in their early days just to stand against the capitalism of the west and the behind-the-scenes funding of war. But did this kind of negative stand against financial manipulators fomenting war in the shadows make him a dangerous man? To certain political powers, apparently, it did. Many have tried to stand against the imperial hubris of numerous countries only to lose their lives in the process.

Both Ernest Hemingway and Pound's protégé, Eustace Mullins, as well as others lobbied for and eventually obtained the release of Ezra Pound. A strong anti-Zionist, Mullins worked in the Library of Congress; and Pound commissioned him to research the world's hidden banking powers. They later published a book called *Secrets of the Federal Reserve.*

It's easy to call Pound and Mullins anti-Semites: there's plenty of evidence. Does this discount their efforts to reveal secret actions of financial power sowing discord between nations? Muckrakers are what the term implies; they take dead water made lifeless by fake optimists and they stir it up. They get oxygen in the system again and they allow fresh water to flow. While a person may have a prejudice in one area, he could have a well of truth in another. In our modern world, if a single prejudice surfaces, it is like the entire soul is dead and we are therefore justified in shutting down their voice entirely. Fake optimists are always at the helm of this kind of action and we need to fire them all.

The great secret is creating a design in which we all can become little muckrakers when needed—and not for the sake of getting attention or for revolution, but for the sake of disagreement with bad ideas. Today we do not challenge bad ideas openly, we push for them. For example, the bad idea of safe spaces replacing free speech on college campuses rejects the vital need for questioning any idea. This is what happens when one person chooses to conserve the value of free speech and another wants to control it in the name of being progressive. The voice of dissent is suddenly removed and the entire spectrum of being open even in one area is shunned.

The genuine optimism of *no*, even when imprisoned by intimidation, confirms a greater *yes*, especially over time. Very few of us are willing to say *no* to the wave of so much *yes* speech that inhibits natural deliberation and open talk. This problem stems from the way the herd's mindset channels agreement with some idolatrous power center without any recourse for individuals to stand and say, "No!" The idolaters too often label the *no* as rebellious rather than (more optimistically) as free.

Ezra Pound presents us with a good example of the optimism of *no*. He knew all too well that packaging the *yes* herd into one corner through financial coercion was part of the dictatorship. Those who seek to shut out rebellious disagreement are covering their real intent: to control and eventually change the law for their gain. Such political rigging for personal advantage hides in the cloak of fake optimism.

The worldviews offered by George Orwell's *1984*, Aldous Huxley's *Brave New World,* and Ray Bradbury's *Fahrenheit 451* provide vivid depictions of secret combinations of state and corporate power sowing discord to create a crisis, which is a practice employed to give the state more centralized power to shut down voice and disagreements. Pound suffered from this worldview and fought against it, even with certain prejudices in tow. His efforts later became known as the modern conspiracy movement, the heretics of our time. Even as I write this massive censorship is taking place across multiple social media platforms. They are removing, often without cause, muckrakers, dissenters and free minds. We call this a technocratic elite trying to control the world. Mention something like this in the open and you are relegated to a conspiracy theorist, a deliberate term used to intimidate questions, disagreements, and hard facts from surfacing into the social consciousness.

Discourse and Secret Intent

The alternative media alone can tell the truth while traditional media is still controlled. Traditional media may imply that there's wrongdoing somewhere, but alternative media will rebel and challenge traditional media's assertions.

Traditional mainstream media has gradually morphed from telling the truth to telling lies; but alternative media can lie, too, especially when we don't fact-check or force more clarity. In either case, we are the blind led by the blind until both fall into the ditch.

If we restore open autonomous discussion, rather than letting any media control every discussion, we can get away from the political imposters who control us. Here's the truth: politics is what happens in secret while culture is what happens in the open. The more widespread we can make this truth, the closer we will come to supporting natural leadership and less political posturing. We might even figure out new technologies to properly open leadership to the entire community.

Consider the trends in media over the past two hundred years. Our future might surprise us all. (See **Figure 5-1**.)

Fig. 5-1 Trends of Media

Complacency	Courage	Control	Conviction	Civil	Common
Oral Traditions	Print Media	Broadcast Media	Alternative Media	Open Media	Consensual Media
Old stories retold over and over by approved authority with no questions allowed.	A burst of freedom at the start that quickly fell into the hands of central control. We read only what is printed and politically correct.	Centrally controlled corporate funded We receive only what is reported and approved by the owners	Whatever the new media personality wants to say in paid sponsor or viewer supported commentary.	Open volunteer reporting and headless structure Not funded.	Organized by common consent in modular form A purely decentralized model. Media operates as both a platform to communicate and to make decisions. Owned by members.

Opposite from the encouraging optimist is the intimidator, and when the intimidator refuses to hear "no," our social discourse is subject to following what the manipulated majority decides. There are indeed far too many people with too much political power and influence, people who are propped up by advanced academic degrees and the financial backing of industries and large corporations. When we centralize power in one authority or in the limited access of just a few, we engender the ultimate intimidating optimist.

Bureaucracies represent very small numbers of people, but no matter how important their supposed rhetoric for social good, they're still bureaucracies because they limit our voices. All voice of dissent is centralized and allowed by just a few, the rest must step in line.

Children can tell lies about their siblings to discredit them with their parents. Likewise, bureaucracies operate with secrecy and tell tales to sow discord behind the scenes. For the first time in American history, we are now aware of the Deep State, a vast network of backscratchers, mutual admiration cliques, and social protectionism. Like a teacher's union with no vision for better education, the collective works in perfect synergy for everyone's self-interest.

We fail to recognize this hideous group-think removed from outside dissent because we cannot prove the motive for their actions, and we are intimidated by it and therefore follow the established rule or the authoritative power. Fake optimism pushes out lies while killing encouragement for revealing them. For the most part, the fake optimism of the bureaucrat follows some social alignment to an implied social good. If we challenge the fake optimist, he'll manipulate us to feel that we are against the good—when our real goal is to expose his secret intent. When you hear someone trying to reveal a secret intent, hire them. They are genuine optimists daring to get to the bottom of something.

Determining the Truth

The voice of the optimistic "no" in the presence of an evasive and hidden motive appears paranoid because the majority of people don't see any hidden intent. Some of us may know instinctively that something's wrong, but we can't define what that is. When people like Ezra Pound reveal secret motives, we don't see what he sees and we call them conspiracy theorists and undercut their free dissent. President Dwight Eisenhower was such a person. He dared to warn American's of the military-industrial complex, a powerful union of defense contractors and the armed forces working in lockstep to advance their own self-interests with almost no outside voice of disagreement.

Fake optimists are very hard to challenge because they judge the "no!" as an attack on their "good." They use this deflection as a cover to hide a different intent. Most people are caught up in the *appearance* of good and don't see any underlying motives.

We're told that if we cannot put up with a little politics in life, we're bound to fail. We delight in some action movies because they show how the villain seems initially to be good, sometimes more so than the hero. The hero is a simple person and overcomes the deceit, showing himself to be the better of the two. We enjoy it because we see the truth. We're unable to deal with it in real life, so we welcome it in fiction.

The typical action movie, for example, becomes our canvas for the struggle between good and evil and we like to see the fake optimist get his due for making evil play the false role of good. In real life, however, things aren't as clear, and we don't see the deception. This happens because in real life we measure evil by destruction rather than deception and secret maneuvers.

This is why we can't see the fake optimist coming before it's too late. We confront murder, rape, and crime, but are disinterested in seeing the heart of deception, denial, and coercion. We rarely admit that the supposed good out there represents evil in sheep's clothing. Just as a child has a difficult time seeing an abusive parent, we likewise want acceptance and so we overlook the deception so prominent in our lives. Like the abused child, we live in darkness, thinking that abuse is love.

Determining the truth is a difficult process, and most people avoid looking for it because the truth is best revealed with the help of more than one person.

For example, there is nothing better for keeping freedom alive than a twelve-person jury determining the truth by unanimous consent. In this closed environment, each person is forced to endure long battles where anyone can seize the discussion and demand answers. It is the perfect example of social encouragement and a model every business or community organization can easily adopt. Compare that to the majority that falls into two polarized groups that remain forever separate and never in agreement. The first is the Platonic state (the modern democrat); the second is the Aristotelian individual (the old conservative). Compare them with the encouraging Socratic (independent mind) and you will see that the Socratic mind leaves your agency in place without evasion and without coercion. Notice the traits of encouraging optimists. They show faith in others, their motivation is to inspire others, and their reward is more community discussion. (See **Figure 5-2.**)

Fig. 5-2 Traits of the Encouraging Optimist

Character	Traites
Idolatry	Faith in Others
Intelligence	Glory in Service
Agency	Freedom to Others
Motivation	Inspires Others
Reward	Community Discussion

Neither the Platonic nor the Aristotelian mind will ever encourage you to think, as does the Socratic mind. The real western tradition died with Socrates, and what lived on is a dualistic view, an idea of unnatural opposition that distorts freedom and not a natural opposition that supports consent. Why has this happened? We are stuck with two mindsets that swing between two points without allowing for any additional points of view to flesh out assumptions and bad ideas.

Socrates asked questions that revealed psychological motives, which in turn revealed faulty meanings. This is the true spirit of an encouraging optimist: to find meaning through dialogue. Neither the Platonic idealism of state control nor the Aristotelian isolation of individual liberty is able to let go: both are too eager to opt for more central control for individual gain.

Plato answered the questions and gave up the dialogue; Aristotle defined his terms without it. Neither encouraged in others the Socratic lift of genuine optimism, supported by disciplined and hard-fought meaning obtained through timeless discussion.

While the principled optimist makes a firm *stand* for freedom, the encouraging optimist *lives* it better. It would be good to differentiate between genuine Socratic optimism (that encourages both social and personal responsibility) and a political duality (that divides and concurs). While this will be elaborated more fully in another book titled *The High Road*, a brief dig is helpful now.

Dissolving the Left-Right Paradigm

In both liberal and conservative minds, whether in business or government, leadership and idolatry combine into a political control model. A political control model is a vertical hierarchy governed by adulation engineering to protect one's position. Fake optimists thrive in this environment.

On the other hand, genuine optimists avoid idolatry for authority, which is the same as avoiding *all* political environments. This explains why we have such disappointing leadership in government, education, religion, and business. Genuine optimists don't advance in any political system because these systems don't allow for discussion and open questioning. They are governed by self-protectionism.

Just look at the loss of social discourse that we once had in the past: for example, the idea of connecting freedom to having a voice in social discourse was almost synonymous in many of the first colonial agreements, charters, ordinances and local constitutions that came before the U.S Constitution. In the *Cambridge Agreement* of December 24, 1632, every person was required to meet every second Monday of every month at the town meeting house after the ringing of the town bell. Those who didn't make a personal appearance, or those who failed to stay until the meeting ended, were required to pay twelve pence. If not paid by the next meeting, they paid double.

In *The Massachusetts Bicameral Ordinance* of March 7, 1644, legislators constructed a two-house legislature in which magistrates on one side and deputies on another side passed bills to each other until both houses reached full consent. Consider the power of that model and compare it with today's typical county commission of three or maybe five members, or a city council with five to seven members, or school board with the same or less. There are many examples of greater involved consent in the past than in our limited and centralized control today.

Even in *The Watertown Covenant* of July 30, 1630, the members of the community enacted a promise to enter into a sure covenant to renounce all idolatry and superstition.[1] What would happen if a community decided to renounce all worship for authority and consequently all idolatry for the same? Once we renounce our desires for authority over us, we begin to imagine a world without the constrictions of a left-right paradigm. The minute you hear people trying to advocate for a better world where greater open voice replaces the typical organizational chart of power and authority, hire them fast. They will be the tool for creating a thriving culture and greater productivity will surface.

Adding Value

I recall attending a *Meet the Experts Luncheon* in which several community business owners spoke about their education, wealth, and business achievements. One entrepreneur stood up in the back of the room and said rather forcefully that he could not get any investors for his business idea. He pushed forward nonetheless and advised all the new entrepreneurs in the room to "go it alone." His true guts and passion showed, for better or worse, and this seemed more optimistic and genuine than the experts who seemed more distant, unapproachable and well connected to the same. The real difference with encouraging optimists is an eagerness to add value and express meaning with great passion, rather than remain aloof in the protection of their positions.

To add value and be honest in a political world seems awkward, but to stand at a distance and add nothing protects one's place and only gives the appearance of knowing something. Hire the first and fire the second.

You'll find two personalities in any organization, one that thinks of taking or controlling value and the other that thinks of adding value. The taker always disguises himself with something smooth and good but that's rarely effective. This sets the fake optimist apart from the genuine optimist who has nothing to disguise. Let me give an example.

The opportunity came to pitch a business idea in front of five venture capitalists at a speed-pitch competition. (This is a situation in which new business ideas are presented to investors.) There were over a hundred small business owners in the auditorium along with four finalists on stage, filtered down from eighty applicants.

I delivered a four-minute pitch, after which one of the judges stood up and said, "Do you know who I am?"

"No," I said.

He explained that he was the principal investor in a business venture similar to the business idea I pitched, but he claimed to have lost millions in the deal. "I strongly suggest you rethink your business model," he said to me. The first thought that came to me was, "You don't know me and I am not you."

Did this businessman understand the power of encouragement? Did he forge a relationship and a new bond? Of course not. All four contestants stood in the hallway to thank the judges… and this judge walked by with head turned away. This is the first thing to watch out for when it comes to false optimists who pretend to care with their tough love. They always walk away from real human interaction, and they seldom add value.

I was left standing and looking dejected in front of established business owners. What you will find is that genuine optimists live through situations that are worse than this, and the only way out is to encourage others. Some faith in yourself helps too.

Just because you rise from a bad situation and achieve great success on another day doesn't make you a genuine optimist. It just means you're stubbornly blind and won't listen to criticism. This type of rugged individualism, assumed to be optimistic, makes the mistake of being isolated. When you meet people like this for the first time, it's as if they are an elitist in their optimism, explosive in energy... but too far away to touch. Their vision knows best, and they remain alone, self-absorbed, defensive, and unable to work toward consensus with others. In the long run, they never scale their success beyond a certain point because they never exercise faith in the structured freedom of common consent. Encouraging optimists do and they build powerful organizations and thriving cultures, until one day when it is sold. Self-absorbed visionaries who do not invest in the added value of others never advance their ideas beyond a certain point. Their self-absorption turns to self-destruction.

Jim Collins has proven this point in his highly researched book *Good to Great*, which by the way was produced from a multi-year team effort. In this book, he identifies what he calls level five leaders.

No matter how visionary leaders may be, they'll never see everything. Such a challenge came some time ago with a potential business partner. I asked her, "Do you believe in the team we've put together?"

"Yes!"

"Okay, if so, then are you willing to let decisions be ruled by common consent from all members on the team?"

Her reply startled me. "I don't subject vision to a committee decision."

"So you believe that vision must come first, and it must rule?" I asked.

"Yes: without vision, the people perish," she argued back.

"So you want me to subject my agency to your leadership?" I asked. She smiled back and didn't say anything.

"I'm sorry, but I can't agree to that." We never moved forward as a team despite all our potential. She needed to be in total control and I needed a voice in full consent.

Compare this with an experience I had with Susan Scott, author, and founder of Fierce Incorporated. I listened to her speak at a conference in Las Vegas, and afterward, she quickly grabbed her suitcase and began to head for the door, in a hurry to make a scheduled flight back home to Seattle.

I held out my hand to indicate my appreciation, and to my surprise, she stopped in the aisle, stepped aside, put her suitcase down, and gave me focused and individual attention. She smiled, said nothing, and listened, letting her "silence do the heavy lifting" as she phrases it. She was more real in the aisle than on stage, and that sticks with people for life. We could have been business partners on the spot.

If we don't bring value to others in a real moment-to-moment way, and if we don't support the free agency of others, we're no better than staged performers and intimidating authorities. A genuinely encouraging person can easily trump the most politically skilled intimidator. The key is getting any political person out in the open so the encouraging optimist can ask questions.

The boomer generation defines optimism as the rugged individualism of being stubborn, pushy and even aggressive. This stands in sharp contrast to the parents of boomers who define optimism as reasonable, patient, and considerate.

Just look at the older boomer generation: it has produced some of the worst presidents in U.S. history. Compared to Presidents Reagan and Kennedy, boomer presidents have produced almost no vision for the country, because they're not encouraging, and they are not relational. They're Platonic and linear. They push for central control to avoid any real social consent. All this came to a head when we voted in Trump, a pure-blood-ed encouraging optimist not afraid to say what many in the population were feeling. Trump is a raw independent human being driven to be as close to working people as possible. It goes with being in the construction industry all of his life. If you want to know how things are going on a job site, talk with the plumbers, electricians, framers and concrete guys. Engage with those that most walk by and ignore.

Trump is relational. He is driven to know people in the field. He does not read books, he reads people. Put him in a crowd and he is naturally attracted to police officers, the military, local laborers and people from all walks of life. What many fail to understand is that he is a construction foreman in a business suit, and this has angered the fake world of pandering to power through sophisticated adulation engineering. Trump has done the opposite of what many think a president should do. He shuns the elite just as all construction workers shun the non-value adding developer in a business suit. At his rallies, he shares the stage and invites locals up to speak. He never shuts down discussion or debate that has an honest question, instead, he tosses himself into the fray. He learns more from talking with real people than appealing to power structures.

Look at John F. Kennedy. He was disgusted with secret intents by hidden power structures aimed at obtaining more central control. He was far more aware of coercive intentions than any president since Abraham Lincoln and Andrew Jackson. Consider Kennedy's knowledge of hidden intent that he discussed in his address before the American Newspaper Publishers Association on April 27, 1961. No president since has ever dared to talk so honestly about the hidden agenda of political power.

> The very word "secrecy" is repugnant in a free and open society; and we are as a people inherently and historically opposed to secret societies, to secret oaths, and secret proceedings. We decided long ago that the dangers of excessive and unwarranted concealment of pertinent facts far outweighed the dangers which are cited to justify it. Even

today, there is little value in opposing the threat of a closed
society by imitating its arbitrary restrictions. Even today,
there is little value in ensuring the survival of our nation
if our traditions do not survive with it. And there is the
very grave danger that an announced need for increased
security will be seized upon by those anxious to expand
its meaning to the very limits of official censorship and
concealment....

Today no war has been declared—and however fierce the
struggle may be, it may never be declared traditionally.
Our way of life is under attack. Those who make themselves our enemy are advancing around the globe.

...For we are opposed around the world by a monolithic
and ruthless conspiracy that relies primarily on covert
means for expanding its sphere of influence—on infiltra-
tion instead of invasion, on subversion instead of elec-
tions, on intimidation instead of free choice, on guerrillas
by night instead of armies by day. It is a system which
has conscripted vast human and material resources into
the building of a tightly knit, highly efficient machine that
combines military, diplomatic, intelligence, economic,
scientific and political operations.

Its preparations are concealed, not published. Its mistakes
are buried, not headlined. Its dissenters are silenced,
not praised. No expenditure is questioned, no rumor is
printed, no secret is revealed. It conducts the Cold War, in
short, with a war-time discipline no democracy would ever
hope or wish to match. [2]

As for Ronald Reagan, although he was incapable of
revealing secretive intent, he was an encouraging optimist. His
main concern was focused on protecting the American spirit,
even though he didn't understand the cartel of elite moving the
agenda (as Kennedy understood all too well).

They were both encouraging optimists. Kennedy did it
by revealing the truth and waking people up to the American
spirit. Reagan did it by communicating his love for that same
spirit. As for Trump, he did it by not letting a swamp of protec-
tionists waste it for their gain.

If you don't agree, perhaps you're looking for something more than encouragement. Perhaps you're looking for a third type of optimism, the kind that many in my parents' generation knew best: I call them principled optimists. If we're lucky, we'll see them communicate vital principles that some of us might convert into a technology or a new organizational model to help build lasting cultures of consent with two powers of yes and no fully protected for each individual.

Very few presidents and leaders in power understand the real value of this optimism. The principled optimist may just be the first to define it and the last hope for preserving freedom and advancing a new renaissance, something I call *The High Road* to come.

I am fundamentally an optimist. Whether that comes from nature or nurture, I cannot say. Part of being optimistic is keeping one's head pointed toward the sun, one's feet moving forward. There were many dark moments when my faith in humanity was sorely tested, but I would not and could not give myself up to despair. That way lays defeat and death.

Nelson Mandela

6
The Principled Optimist

I've concluded that genius is as common as dirt. We suppress our genius only because we haven't yet figured out how to manage a population of educated men and women. The solution, I think, is simple and glorious. Let them manage themselves.[1]

-John Taylor Gatto

The Progression of Optimism

As you've probably guessed, a principled optimist is someone who stands for something good. What you may not know is that it takes at least two people to make the stand: one to speak up—and another to *let* that person speak up.

This book is an attempt to take a stand. It all began with a letter that arrived while I was in college. It came from my father and it said, "Dear Son, for some time I have felt that Satan is trying to exalt you."

It's not easy to get a letter—on your birthday and from your father, no less—with that line in it. The letter was a correction, and correction is part of being raised by a principled optimist, a person who is always taking a stand for the most responsible meaning. Principled optimists dig holes in what you think or believe, but they dig to fill that hole with better material. Principled optimists always fill the holes they dig, or even better they let you fill the hole yourself. In either case, the garbage removed can be anything that inhibits responsible action.

Fathers, mothers, managers, and friends all have some sort of responsibility that's all their own. A mother has the responsibility to correct her child, a friend is responsible for correcting a friend, and a boss has the responsibility of correcting an employee.

Accepting correction is never easy or comfortable: this is where the phrase "I stand corrected" comes from. It takes one to correct and one to be willing to accept correction. It's the same as digging a hole and filling it.

If baby boomers had followed this wisdom, they would have left a better legacy behind them. They are instead leaving a vacuum of freethinking filled with empty holes and no examples of filling their holes. I make this observation as the youngest member of that generation. Born in the tail end of 1964, being the youngest boomer has its advantages. It lets you see the mistakes of your older brothers and sisters. It also lets you see the wisdom of your parents that your older siblings failed to see.

For instance, compare Alcoholics Anonymous with campus safe spaces. AA was founded in 1935 by the parents of boomers. Campus safe spaces are a product of boomer mentality that wanted to protect their children yet teach them nothing. Just try and lie to a group of alcoholics and watch them take a mirror up to your nature and not let you get away with it. Then see how easy it is to pull a lie in the company of supposedly marginalized people in a special safe space, where all lies and all victimization are welcome and unchallenged, and where dissenting views are not tolerated. It is understood that we should not tolerate harassment, violence and racist speech, but to reject dissenting views across the board because they trigger discomfort builds weak intelligence unable to stand for something in the open public.

Most of us know that no person exists as an island. What many people don't know is that personal identity progresses from the individual to the family and then out to the community. There is no safe space free from dissent, and yet boomer parents tried to do this with their children and created the modern millennial generation that is untouched and free from any real challenge and free from the scrutiny of dissent. They are typically quiet, uninvolved, void of real genuine questions about life, and their ability to cope is limited by their lack of being challenged. Conversation in the home about anything was never a staple in their formative years—just mostly encouraging praise with no work ethic and the distraction of social media for self-fulfillment.

Many in my generation seemed to miss this understanding of teaching a principled work ethic. All you have to do is see the weakening of community strength across the country and how it has been replaced by more control at greater and greater distances. The idea of community strength is a central principle of my parents' generation while boomers have mostly dug a hole in that idea without ever filling it. Perhaps an entire generation stands to be corrected.

The expansion of the individual into family and then into the community is the inevitable development of genuine optimism. It's what the genuine optimist is pushing for, especially the *principled* optimist. This is why principled optimists never remove anyone's free agency. They just confront you with a neglected principle that might shift your character toward more community involvement and generally more responsibility.

Take the progression of music as a good example and notice how it applies to human progression from individualism toward community living. In music, we progress toward song and symphony. In human life, we progress toward compassion and community. Without a progression of some kind from one principle to another, optimism suffers.

Discord, Harmony and Overtones

Music is a combination of discord, harmony, and overtones. Discord represents different wavelengths, or two adjoining keys on the piano played at the same time. Tap any two adjoining keys on a piano keyboard together, and you'll find the sound unsettling. It causes stress and doesn't diminish smoothly. It sounds more like *"ouwow"* circling in your ear. However, this sound is awakening. It stirs the soul with divergence rather than division. It can be the one sound in an orchestra that makes or breaks a musical progression.

Harmony, on the other hand, is any note played with an audible crest that falls precisely in line with the crest of another note. Some keys match every third crest, some every fifth, seventh, or eighth. Take any key on the keyboard and move up or down the keyboard until you hear that reverberating crest harmonizing the two keys. When you play both at the same time, you have harmony because of two matching waves that crest and trough at the same time. The fewer matches, the less the harmony. Eight keys away is a full octave that starts over in the matching of crests and troughs.

Finally, we have overtones, subtle bits of harmony that are sympathetic and ride on the back of a stronger harmony. They add variety to the complete musical array. Overtones are like harmony from a different place on the keyboard, like an idea or principle in one community that seems to match a similar idea or principle in another. It could be a harmonizing chord on the guitar or any musical instrument working in tandem with the keyboard. Overtones are everywhere if we look for them.

Essentially, we have harmony and discord, with the occasional overtone. In music, we call this a rich sound. In human language, it's called optimism, the full array of every voice working to settle on a focused vision. There is disruption at moments yet given enough time these differences work out.

Like music, genuine optimism grows out of the community but diminishes in the state and often into larger organizations. The larger the population gets, the more diminished the optimism. Like a rich sound in music, honest optimism diminishes the further the distance traveled. The greater the body of people in which optimism is expressed, the greater its political hypocrisy. This is the hole the boomer generation has dug for itself.

Discord in small localities is quickly corrected by harmony. If the dissent has a very strong harmonic, it'll smooth out any phony optimist in power. In large cultures, the power structure promotes more discord by getting everyone to harmonize without their consent to become part of it. The only way we can maintain true harmony comes from allowing dissent at the most local level. If it has harmonic value, it will overcome discord. If not, it'll dissipate quickly against discussion promoting a stronger harmony.

Education reform is a good example. Too often we have a federal mandate imposed across the nation to test students to quantify teaching results. Teaching to the test becomes the new measure of quality and good teachers leave the profession in the same way genuine optimists leave political environments. With no means to dissent at the local level against an imposing larger mandate without local consent, our cultures are filled with more discord than true harmony.

If you want to understand this problem in education, read John Taylor Gatto's *The Underground History of American Education* and then read his book *A Different Kind of Teacher*. Gatto had trust in families and in neighborhoods and individuals to make sense of the important question. As said in one of his last Tweets before his death in 2018, "What is education for? If one community answers differently from what you might prefer, that's really not your business, and it shouldn't be your problem." Keeping consent as close to individuals, families, and the community is essential for keeping incentive, free agency, and innovation alive. And when they have these fully intact, they are welcome to add value, and adding value in your community is the purest expression of optimism. Shut down this invitation to add value and we have a serious cultural problem.

Dissent against overreaching power increases the potential for local harmony. However, when evil is packaged as good, dissent is too easily marginalized to the far side of a nuisance. We have created safe spaces with no innovation, no creativity, and no challenge to make the world a better place.

Waking to Fake

The world has become so polarized with two opposing parties of discord that we've lost local common ground. Just look at our political climate, in which the progressive liberal wants to solve everything through state and global control, with the end being a unipolar world government. At the same time, the neo-conservative wants to give up liberty in the name of security, but with intent to establish the same grand central control model.

Once upon a time, we argued about federalist responsibility versus individual rights. Now we have a two-headed monster, one side wanting to take all responsibility for our social good and the other side wanting to take all rights for our protection. We think that rights and responsibility are equally separate like two teams on a rope in a game of tug of war. We are forever fighting between statism for all good and a police state for all security. We will never find harmony in people serving and protecting each other locally. The unity of both must come from the consent best originated in a community, which is the best source for harmony because it's the only place where every person's two powers of yes and no can scale with little dissolution. Community is the only place where discord and harmony can exist together.

The problem with a polarized political world favored by fake optimists is that they cannot play harmony with words. They regurgitate slogans and platitudes inherent in their selfishness and idolatrous need to control the masses. When compared to irrational optimists showing *idolatry* in their denial, the principled optimist shows *faith* in the truth. This faith in truth eventually leads to the only true principle strong enough to protect all genuine optimists; it is the principle of common consent. It is the only way to help others see what they cannot see on their own. Common consent is not a safe space that limits discord. It welcomes it and at the same time is structured in smaller bodies to work toward a unanimous agreement. See **(Figure 6-1).**

Fig. 6-1 Traits of the Principled Optimist

Character	Trates
Faith	Faith in Truth
Intelligence	Glory in Vision
Agency	Ask Questions
Motivation	Prophetic Insight
Reward	Ideal Consent

Michael, a close friend, is a warm-hearted believing optimist who touches lives for good. He called last night to talk. After an hour on the phone, he told me of his wife's surgery; doctors removed a cancerous portion of her lower intestine. He explained in detail the difficulties this brought into their lives. He spoke with a forced positive attitude that believed in pushing through and enduring to the end. I have known for many years he is a believing optimist while I am a principled optimist. "Are you online?" I asked.

"No," he responded. "I have dyslexia." Apparently, years before in his youth, he was told he had dyslexia and he accepted this as his identity.

From Michael's point of view, all he knew was how to be a loving and kind man, to touch lives for good. He was a believing optimist locked in one place with no progress. He lived to support his family and wife and to endure almost anything, even great loss and sorrow, with an almost stoic compassion fueled by depressed humility. However, can we say this is optimistic? Maybe, if it touches others—but not if it fails to lift Michael himself. Will he ever stand and say no, to force a better yes? Will he ever progress toward encouragement and principle? Is life an endured process imposed by fate, or do we act on our own? To the outside world, endurance through life seems optimistic, but never from inside our own hearts. This is why I asked if he is online. Is he researching to find answers or alternatives to heal his wife? Is he investigating what the doctors say or is he taking what they say at face value?

When we're emotionally depressed, it's hard to keep fighting to get more out of life or to get better information. This is the real test of optimism. Optimism is made of better stuff than a surrendered humility that handicaps believing optimists. It doesn't inspire them to express the optimism of no in exchange for a greater understanding of what is available in life.

This is why optimism must be like the progression of music that we make rather than a single note played repeatedly. Optimism must grow from belief to encouragement and then to principle—or, in the reverse, from principle to encouragement and then to belief. Both directions are paths of progression from one good position to another good position. This is how good principle is eventually formed. The minute we jump to state, federal, corporate and international organizations, we lose this progressive capacity as individuals. Retaining as much power and voice locally is both conservative and liberal, a perfect harmony. The best music we can create happens in smaller organized bodies where it is easier to incorporate discord and overtones with harmony.

Look for a coming genuine *High Road* in this direction and not in the direction of fake optimists by central planning elitists.

Middle Axis of Meaning

If each of us was to name the most humble and the most genuine person we know, and if we had to choose just one to emulate, most of us would choose the most genuine. The genuine gives all of us something more to aspire to than just the humble strength to endure. Genuine can be a little more discord at times but it naturally progresses toward the community. Does this reject humility as a stand-alone quality? No! Humility for those choosing to leave the practice of being fake in their optimism is essential. In this, they progress toward genuine optimism for the first time. To progress and to endure are different expressions. The first aligns with optimism and the latter tightens his or her teeth with a half-smile.

The intention isn't to debase humility. The only intention is to show clearly that in times of great challenge, and against great odds, optimism is the act of building. Humility can be useful: it's sometimes a much-needed demolition. Humility brings down what tries to command and control everything. We've already talked about the revolution of no that promotes a greater confirmation of yes. *Responsibility is both revolution and confirmation, and when we have both yes and no in equilibrium and as locally as possible, we define this as freedom.*

It's like looking at a scale with weight for yes on one side and weight for no on the other side. The reason why one side tends to outweigh the other is that we take our eye off the middle axis of meaning, which the Socratic relational mind finds in *The Tree of Life*.

The Principle of the Tree of Life

There's a big difference between opposition and separation. With opposition, two or more views can stay in the discussion. With separation, two or more views eventually become polarized while rejecting any outside perspective.

This idea of separation began with the Judeo-Christian story of Adam and Eve. In this story, God planted two trees in the Garden of Eden and commanded Adam and Eve to eat from the Tree of Life, but not to eat from the Tree of Knowledge of Good and Evil. Eve decided otherwise and ate from the Tree of the Knowledge of Good and Evil. Adam followed and the Lord banished both from the garden, thus beginning what Christians refer to as original sin.

What's the difference really between these two trees? We know that good and evil exist as a separation, a kind of division between bitter and sweet, joy and sorrow, pleasure and pain. This isn't the case with the Tree of life. The Tree of Life is a natural opposition, what we see between male and female, the ideal and the real, justice and mercy, reason and intuition. The opposition in these does not divide and separate, they show equilibrium and unity when equally balanced.

The wisdom of the universe perhaps meant for us to sustain a natural opposition in all things found in the Tree of Life, rather than an unnatural separation in the Tree of Knowledge of Good and Evil. This may explain why we're as polarized as any other people in history. Only at special times have we shown otherwise. Perhaps that's our trial: to learn to choose meaning through more open consent after experiencing so much meaning imposed by authority. If this were the case, then true meaning obtained through open discourse and not authoritative rule is our salvation.

Does opposition incorporate evil? Natural opposition is the optimism of "no" that's allowed to germinate a clearer meaning—and a total consent for "yes." So, to answer the question, evil cannot survive in this environment. With continued freedom to say no, natural opposition sustains meaning and real progress. This has absolutely nothing to do with incorporating evil. It has everything to do with freedom. This is how principled optimists think, everything is condensed to clear and responsible meaning so that evil cannot usurp control with fake optimism or centralize power with outright force.

Evil works to shut down the freedom of dissenting ideas against itself: it's not progressive. Only natural opposition allows for a greater vision of more good because it allows for dissent voiced throughout the process. Evil doesn't allow for this. It can exist in division and more separation, the tools of fake optimists.

Freedom can exist in a state of opposition, like what's found between a believing optimist and a principled optimist, or among all three genuine optimists. It's never in a duality of good and evil, such as between an irrational optimist and a principled optimist. This kind of division is not a natural opposition. Evil does not make you a better person. Only natural opposition does this.

Both freedom and responsibility belong in a natural state of opposition rather than in a state of division (as found with good and evil). Black-and-white notions of reality support more duality and more division rather than an opposition that progresses naturally toward the consent within the community. In a natural state of opposition, it is difficult for evil to take hold.

When we support separation, evil takes more power through discord, division, and deception. Evil then roots itself more deeply into our social conscience, creating more division and more separation. If you don't believe this, consider the two camps of public discourse that have ruled governments throughout history.

The first camp is the Platonic. Driven from the top down, this centrally controlled model commands blindly and controls without responsibility. It's the more pervasive of the two. The only reason we call it *public* is that it employs the semblance of openness in public discourse by using a majority-rule democratic process. Just about every institution employs this first model, including religious institutions, governments, businesses, and non-profit organizations. It focuses primarily on power centers of control and suffers from the worship of authority by position and not leadership. It's linear in logic.

The second camp is the Socratic, driving the open forum and unanimous consent—and, in rare situations, a supermajority rule. This process seems to take a longer time for decisions making, but it's also less prone to corruption. The Socratic decentralizes. It is relational. It begins with first principles and continues in logic to maintain responsible action is taking place. It asks questions not to jar or frustrate but to establish meaning. It places epistemology (how we know) before metaphysics (what we know as real).

Models for the Socratic include the jury system, our constitutional convention, the Knights of the Round Table, the Magna Carta, the Charter of Liberties, the Iroquois Five Nation Confederacy, and the Swiss Cantons. The Socratic model founded on the highest level of consensus from the people is often associated with the classical social contract. It empowers people and not the idolatry of individuals over people. It is relational in logic. It trusts in systems and processes that unite everyone's voice and not people and power that centralizes power in one voice.

What Role Will You Play?

The big question is this: is public discourse entering a new renaissance? If so, what role will you play? Will you continue with more Platonic king-making models of central control or will you decentralize power with more voice and greater consent of the people? In business, we scale for growth. In education, we scale for learning. Why not scale the government for more dissent? Shifting the paradigm like this may just be the answer to launching a new renaissance.

Letting people manage themselves with greater room for dissent while progressing toward community consent, this will solve the problem of divisive separation found with political correction. With less division, we can all challenge one another freely rather than submit to the supposed expert, authority, media panel, or political correction. Rather than separate the people from a panel of experts often selected for purely biased reasons, why not scale the opportunity for all to be experts? Rather than a panel that appeals to the worship of authority, why not have a convention that advances ideas? **See Figure 6-2**

Fig. 6-2 The Center of the Socratic Eye

Platonic	Socratic	Aristotellian
God of Force	God of Responsibility	God of Logic
Liveral	Inquiring Mind	Conservative
The Ideal	The Meaning	The Real
Position is Power	Wisdom is Power	Knowledge is Power
Word of Truth	Spirit of Truth	Light of Truth

Freedom is what the principled optimist struggles to stand for in a world stuck in the duality of good and evil—a purely political and linear construct that believes we are either born sinners or born selfish. It never believes that we are born good or that we are born free. A natural opposition allows for greater beliefs that lift rather than support only those beliefs that demand more control. It is not too late for the boomer generation to properly fill the hole of self-love they dug for themselves and scale that self-expression into greater local responsibility.

Many times in college, high school, and even Sunday school, teachers are deliberately selective in what they include in the lecture. The teacher obviously cannot include everything, but to shut out the content of a discussion that will help better define complex terms means the teacher is controlling freedom. The teacher does it to save time and get through the lecture, but why not allow more time to talk? Why not have a class that works like a jury—and not let the class end until there is a consensus? Wow, what kind of education would that be? Is this what the Tree of Life is about, granting more time for natural opposition? A greater consensus is better than backroom deals made to prevent questions or statements?

In 2002 the Oakland A's played their longest baseball game ever. It took over 19 innings and didn't end until six hours and thirty-two minutes later! Baseball has become an American pastime because of the timeless nature of the sport. We need more timeless approaches to life and less sudden-death elimination. The first is genuine optimism and the latter is fake optimism.

The Tree of Life is a renaissance of people willing to incorporate natural opposition into their lives. They're willing to take more time to work things out with the full consent of everyone involved. When this is allowed, the vision that surfaces will astound many of us.

Small Example

I teach part-time at a local university. I gave a final to an entire class of freshman and sophomores enrolled in an inter-personal communications course. Their challenge was to come together as the whole class with a unified understanding of the problem of human disconnection and to then offer a unique solution. It took several meetings off campus and many hours of discussion. Ideas were offered and they were batted down because the students did not have a wide body of consent. If they agreed to decide based on a majority rule, they would have settled for a usual solution with no real insight or innovation. Eventually, the entire class agreed on one thing, something they called the Trailblazer Dream Tree.

The Trailblazer Dream Tree (TDT) is a cultural outreach of students who create connected memories by being a catalyst for countless gatherings with the unstated intent of befriend-ing students. As part of the outreach, they will have an inviting place on campus called the dream tree. On this tree members of the club will place ribbons. The three different ribbons will be red for dreams realized, blue for dreams created, and white for dreams saved.

Included at the site will be a unique billboard indicat-ing a contact for suicide prevention and other resources, plus an events calendar for everyone interested in attending a dream club activity. Once members join, they become part of a rising tide that lifts all ships, and they become members for life. The mission of the club is to inspire and save dreams. The hidden motive is to build a thriving culture that is sustained over many generations.

After twenty-five years of teaching part-time on several college campuses, I have witnessed too many important services become compartmentalized into a counseling center, an advise-ment office, a diversity director, a career center, or a multi-cul-tural department, but never a living breathing culture that thrives on its own without authority in charge. The challenge we have is to create models that invite others to add their value. Instead, we have models that control what value is added and where value is spent.

Reconnection and Consent

This problem of social disconnect at odds with social consent is not something new. Monarchs or presidents at the top of a corporate ladder typically want to shut down progressive freedom because there are too many free-floating ideas for them to control. When there are too many voices, controlling minds gather together to devise plans to centralize control, and it is done in the name of efficiency.

Fake optimists want freedom, but not for everyone. They even have the gall to call their plans progressive—when they are anything but progressive. In the tyranny of excessive control, taking freedom away works to the tyrant's advantage, as long as they lie and call their ideas progressive.

Yet it's not progressive to centralize the freedom of dissent. Historically, progress is always on the side of decentralizing freedom. Compare our modern social justice movement to the Magna Carta. Written in 1215 as a deliberate attempt by nobles, barons, and the wealthy to put themselves on equal ground with the king, the Magna Carta was given to the king by his subjects in an attempt to limit and decentralize his power. With social justice, it is an imposition pushed on people without their consent. Not everyone has equal footing. It is just a social correction for their own good. It is fake and not genuine.

Over the centuries, the progress of freedom wanted more since more people demanded the same freedom to stand against the king, and thus came the American Declaration of Independence, the Constitution, the Bill of Rights and many other similar documents. All these enlarged the progress of freedom. Over time, though, the voice of the people became threatened. In the minds of some is the assumption that all these voices are too impossible to pull together, and so the only solution is to centralize control to make it more efficient. We call this fascism, socialism, state communism, and we even call this popular democracy and crony capitalism. These progress toward the narrow constriction of collective hierarchies. They do not progress toward the creation of thriving cultures with more freedom and more local responsibility.

For instance, many call fascism a right-winged radical authoritarian nationalism, but in truth, it is the merger of corporations and government. How else can you centralize so much power without financial support? Fascism is authoritarian elitism. It comes from the plural form of the Latin *fascis*, meaning a bundle of elm or birch rods about five meters in length. In Rome, an ax head was often tied to the bundle with a red strap signifying bundled individuals under the power of one. Mussolini adopted the emblem for his fascist party as a means to unite the people under the state (for a united good), without telling them of the central control given to corporate oligarchs (for their collective profit).

The same follows for socialism, communism and the rest. They all suffer the problem of centralizing power for the limited benefit of a few. Principled optimists see this problem clearly. They see that freedom must progress through natural opposition of each individual in their community, not through separation and division of all individuals under centralized authority.

New Adoption

We must adopt The Tree of Life as our means to genuine optimism and stop eating from the Tree of the Knowledge of Good and Evil, which conquers people through division and separation. The Tree of Life bears the fruit of natural opposition. It is the path of localized common consent that never allows polarization to take place where the uninformed majority support more and more centralized control sold by fake optimists.

Only in natural opposition (which is long, tedious, wide open for disagreement, and slow in arriving at consensus) will freedom decentralize control naturally. The expediency crowd will want to centralize control to get things done quickly; the efficiency crowd will want to limit access by allowing less discussion. Only the genuine crowd will play a timeless game as they progress toward community through the long game called a culture of consent.

Voice in discussion and vote in consent must scale together simultaneously and in very close proximity (the same room), always unanimously and then into the next room by the same means. This is the highest and best principle of human organization that supports genuine optimists.

Even now, we are, with the help of the Internet, the most liberated generation, with wide-open freedom placed before us. Despite this marvelous technology, we've chosen globalism, corporate monopolies, political division, executive fiat, cartels, cabals, and collusion. We have all this voice with no vote connected to that voice.

Fake optimists will often create a crisis to inject and claim more control of our voices: the standing rule for all fake optimists is to never let a good crisis go to waste. The term *crisis* comes from the goddess Isis, whose name in Egyptian means "throne." The "throne" of control that a "crisis" comes from simply divides and conquers the people. Principled optimists have this power to keep meaning clear; they make great leaders because they stay the course and conserve the best agreed-upon understanding that all have. Hire them.

Genuine optimists demand that control become touching acts of belief, mentors of encouragement, and a principle that stands the test of time. Hire them. Without the faith necessary to let freedom flourish in these directions, leaders tend to fear criticism of their decisions and they become fake optimists. Fire them. We find them doing everything in their power to control or spin away dissent and criticism. They cannot help but reveal that they have no vision to come out from behind themselves and into the open conversation.

Leadership today is failing to manage real diverse conversations because it sides with a partisan crowd rather than engage the body of the whole at the most basic level of any organization.

There's no best practice eluding us; there's no dressed-up positive mental exertion and a new rhetoric to go with it. There's only free discussion working toward the highest degree of public consent possible.

A society that conserves the twin powers of freedom in each person in the crowd can only develop in a graduated consensus, with each person having full and independent agency to dissent in his or her group.

The fake optimist, with no working principle of freedom, fears standing in front of those expressing dissent against their control. The risk of losing power is too great. Throughout history, there are more fake optimists directing society than there are genuine optimists appearing on the scene. Because every generation fails to exercise faith in human freedom, we always need to show additional faith. The real battle is about abolishing our idolatry for authority and replacing it with the principle of greater consent taught at every level of civilization.

Common consent is the conservation of responsibility within the most local organization, perhaps the most powerful truth held by a principled optimist.

Faith in Consent

If you think of faith as a positive mental exertion, or some sort of upbeat thinking, a positive attitude then could very well be a fake act if there's no responsibility attached to it. For example, a sales manager can intimidate the entire staff by saying, "You have to think positively if you want to make sales—stop being so negative!" The sales manager is intimidating to cover his fear. He doesn't have faith. The use of intimidation is a sign of dishonesty covered by the cloak of a positive mental exertion. A manager leading the sales staff in faith would say, "We make sales by serving a need, so listen to the words of your clients and find a way to serve that need."

When you're interviewing candidates to hire look for their *meaning of faith*. Faith reveals their view of freedom, and that in turn reveals their individual motives for everything else. If one thinks that doing the honest thing, coupled with hard work, is faith, then responsibility connects to the meaning—and the person is apt to succeed. If the person talks about sales and numbers with no regard for how they achieve those numbers, you have a big problem. A business may have a quick jump in sales with a fake optimist, but it will never sustain that growth. Fake optimists in sales are transaction-driven rather than builders of relationships. With fake optimists, everything at every moment is about making the sale or getting more control and not about building a long-term client base. Put in a proper business sense, you can scale and remain sustainable with genuine optimists but you cannot scale and remain in business with fake optimists.

When it comes to hiring people, the wide spectrum of input from as many people as possible is the best bet. My wife services many big corporations as their realtor. When new candidates come to town, she drives them around looking at homes and communities. What she learns about them with their guard down is amazing. If leaders were smart, they would use many third-party services in the community, not head hunters but real people, to get a better feel of candidates and how they operate. Even the night janitor should get involved in the process.

Think about the difference between "thinking positively" and "taking responsibility." Thinking positively is not something that can be shared. It is too relative to each person. However, taking responsibility is something that can be shared and distributed. The latter is truly in your reach; the former is difficult to grasp. Thinking positively is not a sustainable approach to business. Taking responsibility, on the other hand, is sustainable.

There is only one way to keep the fake optimist from infiltrating the system with fake positiveness and usurping power, and that's the principle of common consent.

We tend to associate responsibility with a pyramid, in which one person at the head makes all decisions. This is a serious error. Responsibility comes when we hold consent in common when more voice is involved.

In Practice

A few weeks ago, my business team interviewed a candidate who would head up the technical side of things and eventually become our chief technical officer. Each person who interviewed him had a completely different experience, and they were not consistently positive. I had a positive feeling, but my other three partners didn't share my enthusiasm. My partners noted the candidate's unwillingness to sacrifice and work hard for the company, plus other issues that had surfaced in the negotiations. It had been easy for me to ignore those issues because of the candidate's skills and experience—*and* the feeling of importance the candidate had given me.

Genuine optimists are quick to see where they can serve. Fake optimists are not service-oriented, and yet they tell you what you want to hear. Fake optimists look for advantages and they are always looking to jockey for a position of control. No matter how talented and experienced they are, they cannot compare with a volunteer willing to give more time and more effort, even with less experience and sometimes no pay.

The only way to attract volunteers with belief, encouragement, and principle is to give them a real voice in the game and to protect the value they add. Fake optimists will want more value in return for less. They will want full control, often giving nobody any voice of consent, and they will manipulate all value under their watchful eye. They will not reveal this openly, which is why you need all eyes on the game to look into their motive, their actions, and get them to talk and engage in discourse. Eventually, someone will see either the fake optimism found in a staged front, intimidation that sounds authoritative, or irrationalism that sounds magical; or they will find something genuine in their belief, how they encourage others or a base principle without hypocrisy.

It's amazing to see how corporations, governments, and even religious institutions have been organized with such centralized control without the invested discernment of others. Why we think this model is good is a sign of our continued idolatry of authority.

However, by building new structures on natural opposition best seen in the practice of common consent as locally as possible in organizations, we support the freedom necessary to create better institutions in education, healthcare, government, and business as well as in community service. In other words, we support a more sustainable approach of taking responsibility and we build more thriving cultures with fewer power struggles.

This idea of freedom built on common consent (where it's within each person's agency to say yes and no) is the foundation of everything that's genuinely optimistic. The problem is that most of us have no idea how first to protect this freedom, and second how to scale it into large groups.

The Conservation of Responsibility

This is where the conservation of responsibility comes into play. It's a principle that protects freedom while at the same time allowing it to scale into very large organizations. It may sound impractical, but it's not. Put into practice it simply means *I alone will not decide who to hire because I do not see everything.* Instead, all team members get to decide. It also means that innovation must flow as freely as vision. So, if vision comes from the top down with almost no hiccups, innovation to make that vision a success must flow up and with no hiccups. There can be no bottlenecks of control that inhibit the free flow of vision as well as innovation. If there are serious bottlenecks, fire them or learn to organize without them.

For instance, a team is better to manage a department than a single person. Stop hiring directors, deans, and department heads and try replacing them with teams, councils, and small groups equally accountable and equally free. Require that they reach common consent and test their outcome but make sure you conserve some of their added value back into their hands. If you think this is nuts, you have never tried it. If you have many in power fight it, you know you have a problem. Anyway, what do you have to lose? Better yet, what do you have to gain? You may have genuine optimists on board who traditionally kept to themselves in fake environments until now.

At Vision Impact Leadership we help organizations decentralize for more voice. We help create more freedom to incentivize more value-added. If your organization is highly political and driven by a rigid hierarchy, and if you are suffering from a lack of innovation and free communication flow, change can happen. It will take some time but eventually, a thriving culture can replace the gridlock of power struggles created by fake optimists. By eliminating controlling positions, you suddenly attract more ideas, more value-adding people, and more free communication. This equals a thriving culture, and this is always genuine.

Principle Footing

The principled optimist stands against the irrational optimist in profound ways. Just the other day a friend sent me an inspirational video to watch online. The speaker, Eduardo Briceno, started with the usual question, "What do you think is required to reach our ultimate goals?"[2] Briceno told the story of Josh Waitzkin, the winner of multiple chess championships. Later, at the age of 21, Josh decided to master martial arts and eventually won several championships in Tai Chi from 2002-2004. The speaker quoted from Josh Waitzkin to explain his success: "The moment we believe that success is determined by an ingrained level of ability, we will be brittle in the face of adversity."

Eduardo Briceno talks about the research of Stanford Professor Dr. Carol Dweck, who realized the differences between a *fixed mindset* and a *growth mindset*.[3] In her book *Mindset: The New Psychology of Success*, a fixed mindset says, "Effort is for the incapable." A growth mindset says "Effort makes me smarter." A teacher with a fixed quality of intelligence says to a student, "You must be smart at this." A teacher promoting a growth quality of intelligence says, "You must have tried really hard."

I sent the video link to my father, the most disciplined principle optimist I know, and I got this reply:

> You can study anything and come up with a formula for success. The real power of achievement is in a group of minds or more than one mind. Other than this, you cannot intellectualize success by any means of assurance. Sportscasters intellectualize sports but fail to consider timing. One succeeds or fails because of some choice he made. Choices make little difference when it is not the right time and the right place.

> I have failed consistently at computer programing. I have no idea how I ever succeeded in any attempt to program before. What I have learned is to focus as locally as possible and stop searching for some answer held by some knowledge base. Things are designed in small packages and tested by the designer. Looking elsewhere, outside of the package, leads to accidental workings that cannot be repeated because of an unknown variable. I thought I had everything working on my web site. In deleting some files related to old failures, I realized the prior successes were automated beyond my knowledge. By going through the simple process intended by the program, by the use of a good video, I was able to do it more simply than before with perfect success.

> Knowing your tools is better than hard work. Knowing how things work is better than positive thinking. Hard work and positive thinking are forms of denial. The only common denominator of success is to know your tools (your people) and your product better than any other person. Fabricating some illusion or thinking someone already has the answer spells failure.

Many researchers on the topic of success do not discuss how to scale the idea of a growth mindset for the community. They always stop at the individual, which is the case with the talk by Eduardo Briceno. It is one thing for an individual to become the best in the world in two competitive events, such as chess and martial arts. It is quite another for a whole group to rise to greater achievement without an individual overseer.

When you scale everything great about the individual into the community or a member into the corporation, you cannot be left with an individual overlord over the whole. The entire organization must move in a growth mindset, like a beehive, as if they are one mind. This is not a collective hierarchy; it is a thriving culture of consent. This is the only model that vitally protects the unique qualities of voice, vote, and value from everyone. This is also the only model that best advances genuine optimists into the leadership of a new renaissance. We call this *The High Road*.

The Staged Optimist

1   Orson Welles on Acting. https://www.youtube.com/watch?v=m1CS_LRfwd4. Also quoted in http://a-bittersweet-life.tumblr.com/post/49785836946/i-think-acting-is-like-sculpture-in-other-words.

2   John Stewart Mill. *On Liberty*. Chapter II Of the Liberty of Thought and Discussion.

3   http://www.washingtonexaminer.com/obama-the-repeal-debate-is-and-should-be-over/article/2547402. Accessed January 24, 2014.

4   Samuel Louis Dael *The Platonic Idiom*. Vision Impact Publishing 2007

5   Marcus Aurelius *Meditations* Book II

Intimidating Optimist

1   http://www.presidentialrhetoric.com/speeches/02.04.05.html. Accessed January 26, 2015.

2   Collins, Jim. Good to Great. Harper Collins. 2001.

3   Scott, Susan. Fierce Conversations. 2002

4   John F Kennedy. "President and the Press." Address before the American Newspaper Publishers Association. April 27, 1961. http://www.jfklibrary.org/Research/Research-Aids/JFK-Speeches/American-Newspaper-Publishers-Association_19610427.aspx

5   Thomas Paine. The Rights of Man.1779.

6   https://www.youtube.com/watch?v=GiPe1OiKQuk. Accessed on January 28, 2015

7   https://www.youtube.com/watch?v=k3bbqlif_eQ. Accessed on January 28, 2015

8   http://en.wikipedia.org/wiki/Marinus_van_der_Lubbe. Accessed on January 28, 2015

9   A slogan popularized by Karl Marx in his 1875 Critique of the Gotha Program.

10   R.J Rummel. Statistics of Democide: Genocide and Mass Murer Since 1900. Center for National Security Law. www.mega.nu/ampp/rummel/note5.htm

11   R.J Rummel. Freedom, Democracy, Peace: Power, Democide and
     War. Introduction. http://www.hawaii.edu/powerkills/

Irrational Optimist

1   Byrne, Rhonda. *The Secret*. 2006.

Encouraging Optimist

1   Colonial Origins of the American Constitution. Edited by Donald S
     Lutz. 1998.

2   http://www.jfklibrary.org/Research/Research-Aids/JFK-Speeches/
     American-Newspaper-Publishers-Association_19610427.aspx,
     Accessed on March 3, 2015.

Principled Optimist

1   John Taylor Gatto. Weapons of Mass Instruction: A Schoolteacher's
     Journey Through the Dark World of Compulsory Schooling.

2   Ted talk by Eduardo Briceno at Ted Manhattan Beach. Accessed
     on February 24, 2015. https://mail.google.com/mail/u/0/#search/
     dean.g.boren%40gmail.com/14bafae70830a01d?projector=1

3   Carol Dweck Ph.D. *Mindset: The New Psychology of Success*.
     2007.